I0824497

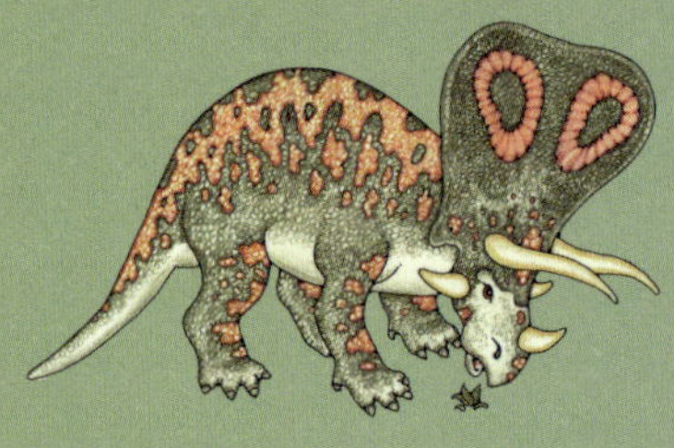

DANDI PALMER has been a professional illustrator for over forty years. She has been commissioned by many publications and organizations including the *Radio Times*, *BBC Focus*, *Prima* and UNESCO.

On her website – www.dandipal.uk – you will find a selection of her work including picture books for children, and science fiction, fiction and supernatural/fantasy stories for adults, written under the name of Jane Palmer on www.booksfromdodo.uk

Also in the *Draw 30* Series:

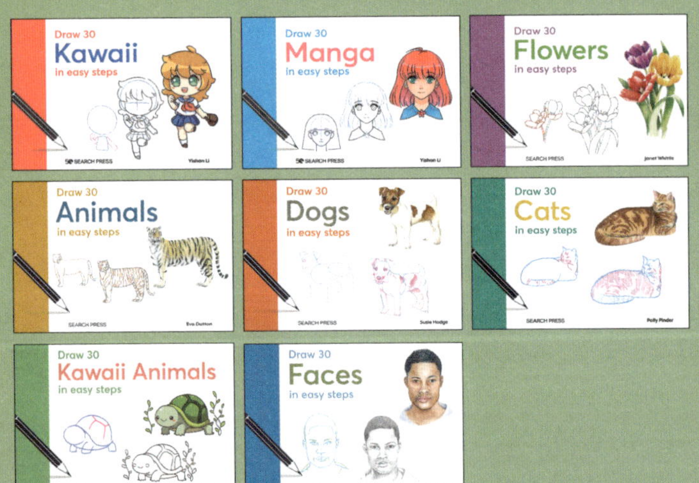

Draw 30 Dinosaurs in easy steps

Dandi Palmer

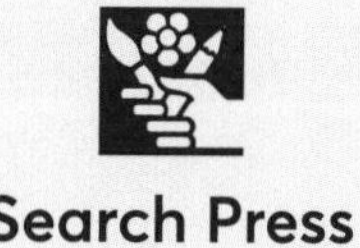

Search Press

About this book

Dinosaurs are brilliant fun to draw! In this book, I'll guide you through simple steps to sketch favourites like Tyrannosaurus, Velociraptor and Stegosaurus, as well as lesser-known creatures like Amargasaurus and Microraptor.

Each drawing begins with basic shapes in one colour, then builds up in a second colour to form the full dinosaur portrait. Once you're happy with the outline, go over the keylines in pen and erase the sketch marks. I've used coloured pencils to bring the extinct to life, but feel free to use whatever medium you enjoy.

With a bit of practice, you'll soon be creating your own prehistoric masterpieces!

The contents

4: Amargasaurus

6: Anchiornis

8: Ankylosaurus

10: Araripesuchus

12: Archaeopteryx

14: Carnotaurus

16: Coelophysis

18: Corythosaurus

20: Deinonychus

22: Dilophosaurus

24: Diplodocus

26: Edmontosaurus

28: Iguanodon

30: Kentrosaurus

32: Microraptor
34. Ornithomimus
36: Orodromeus
38: Oviraptor
40: Parasaurolophus
42: Protoceratops
44: Saltasaurus
46: Spinosaurus
48: Stegoceras
50: Stegosaurus
52: Styracosaurus
54: Torosaurus
56: Triceratops
58: Troodon
60: Tyrannosaurus
62: Velociraptor

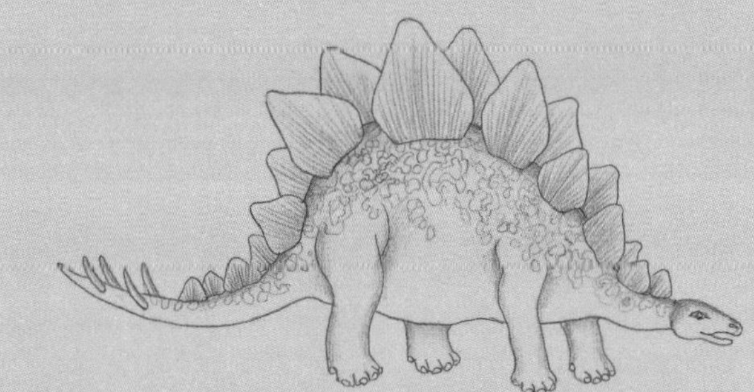

The Drawings

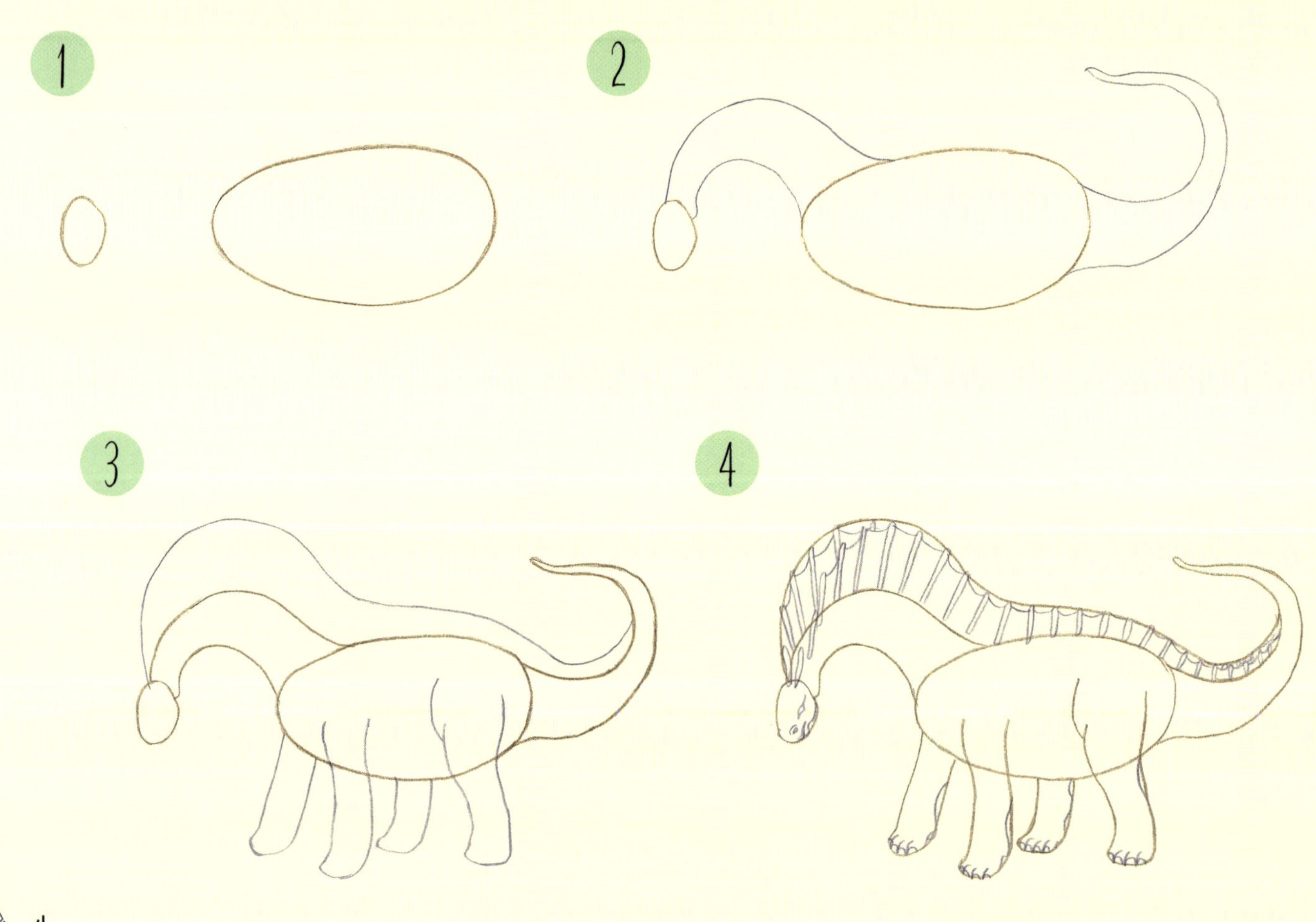
1
2
3
4

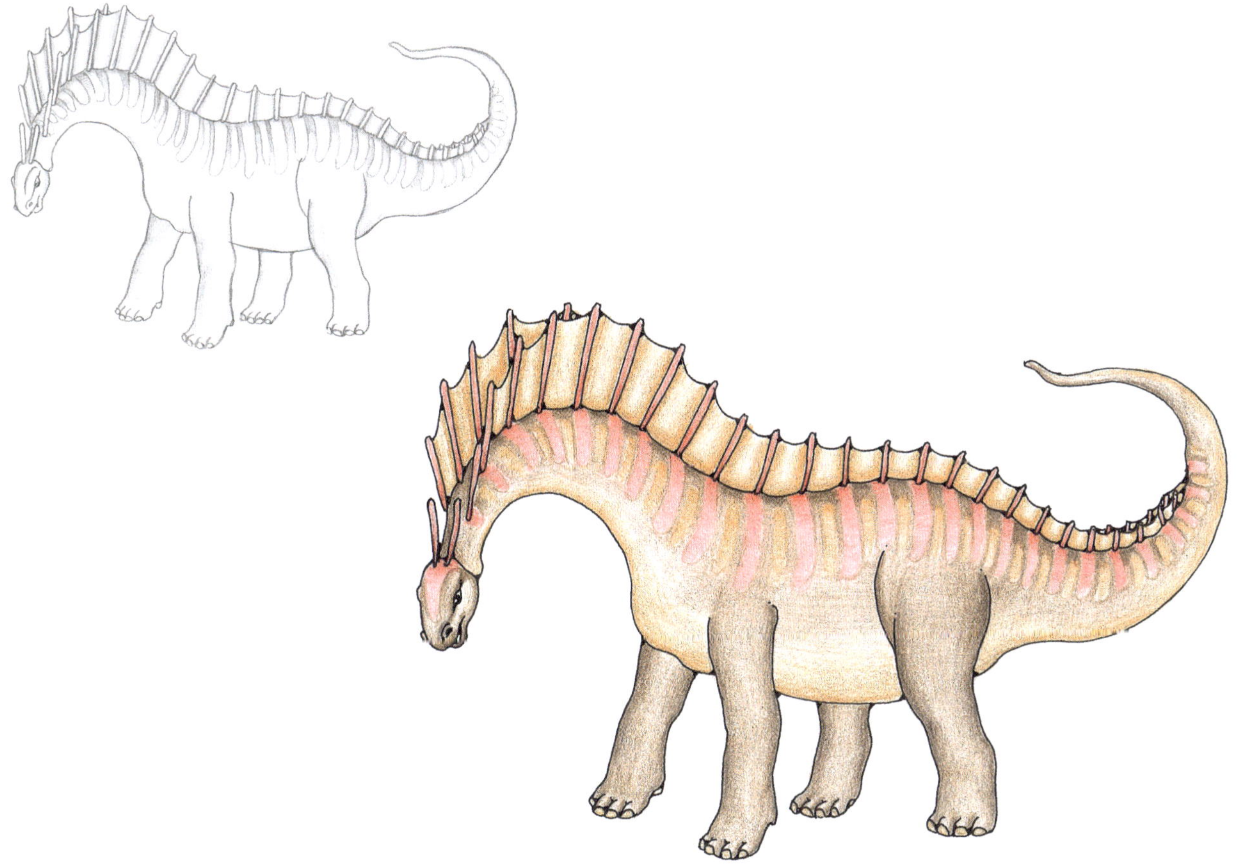
5

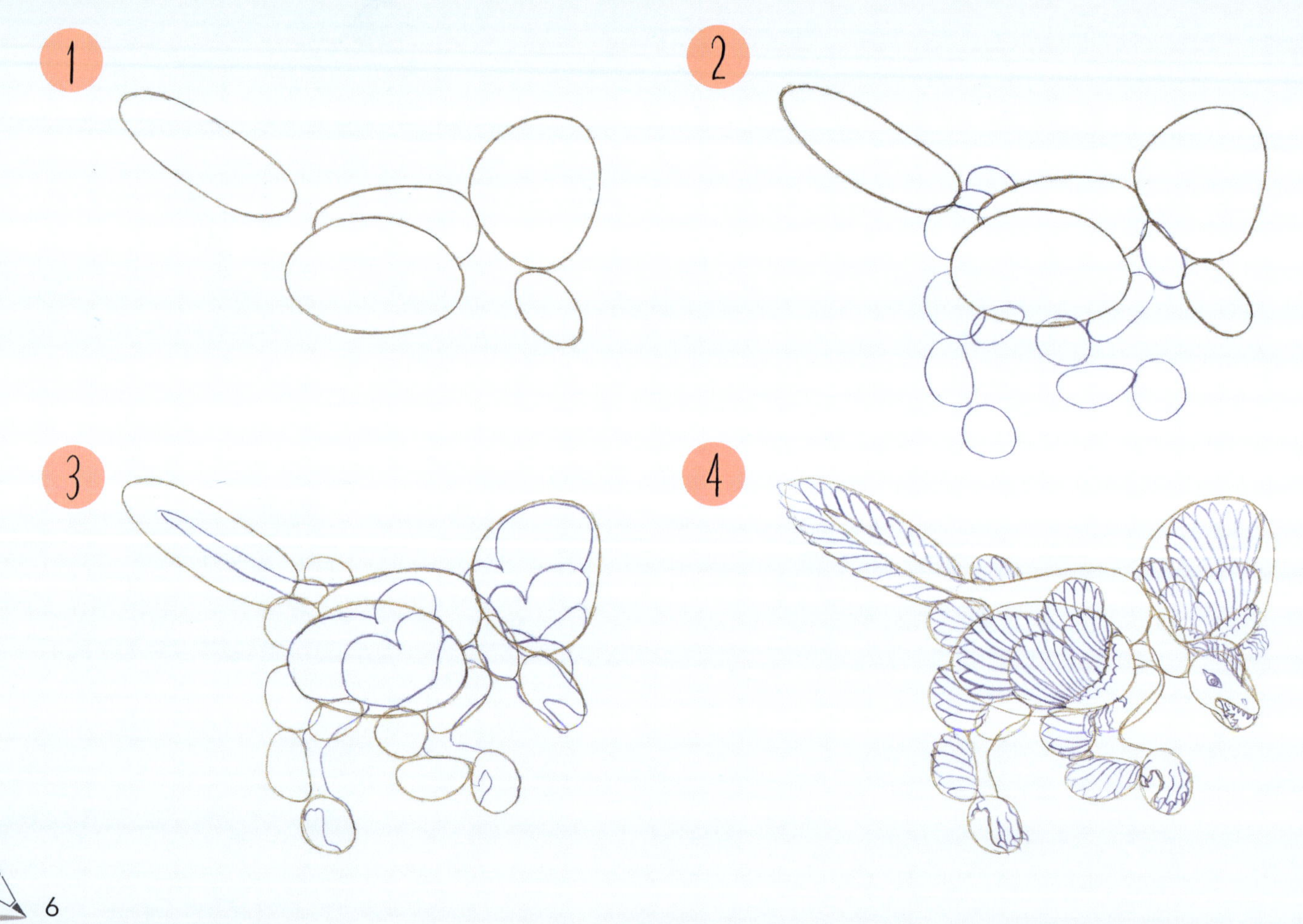
1
2
3
4

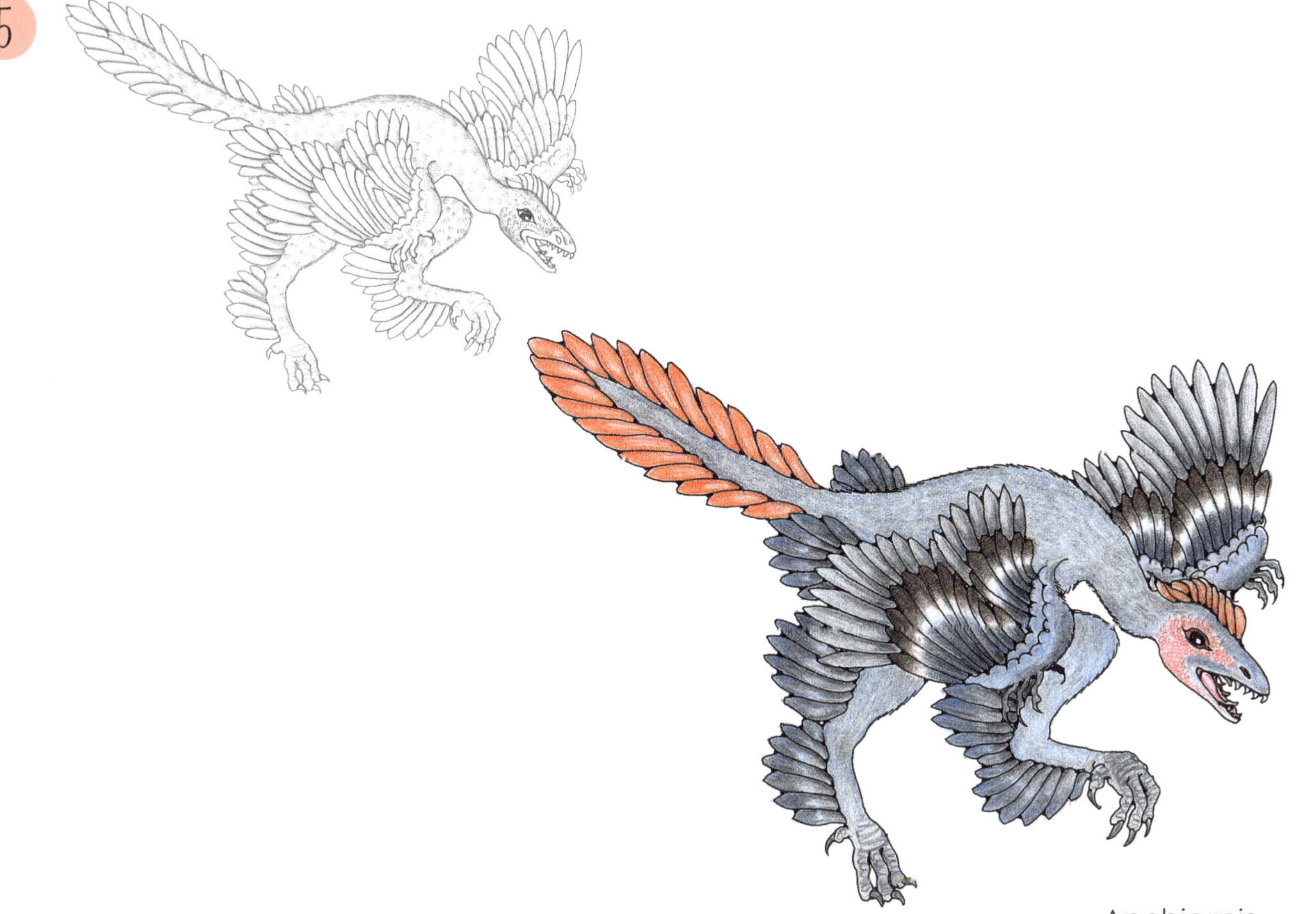
5

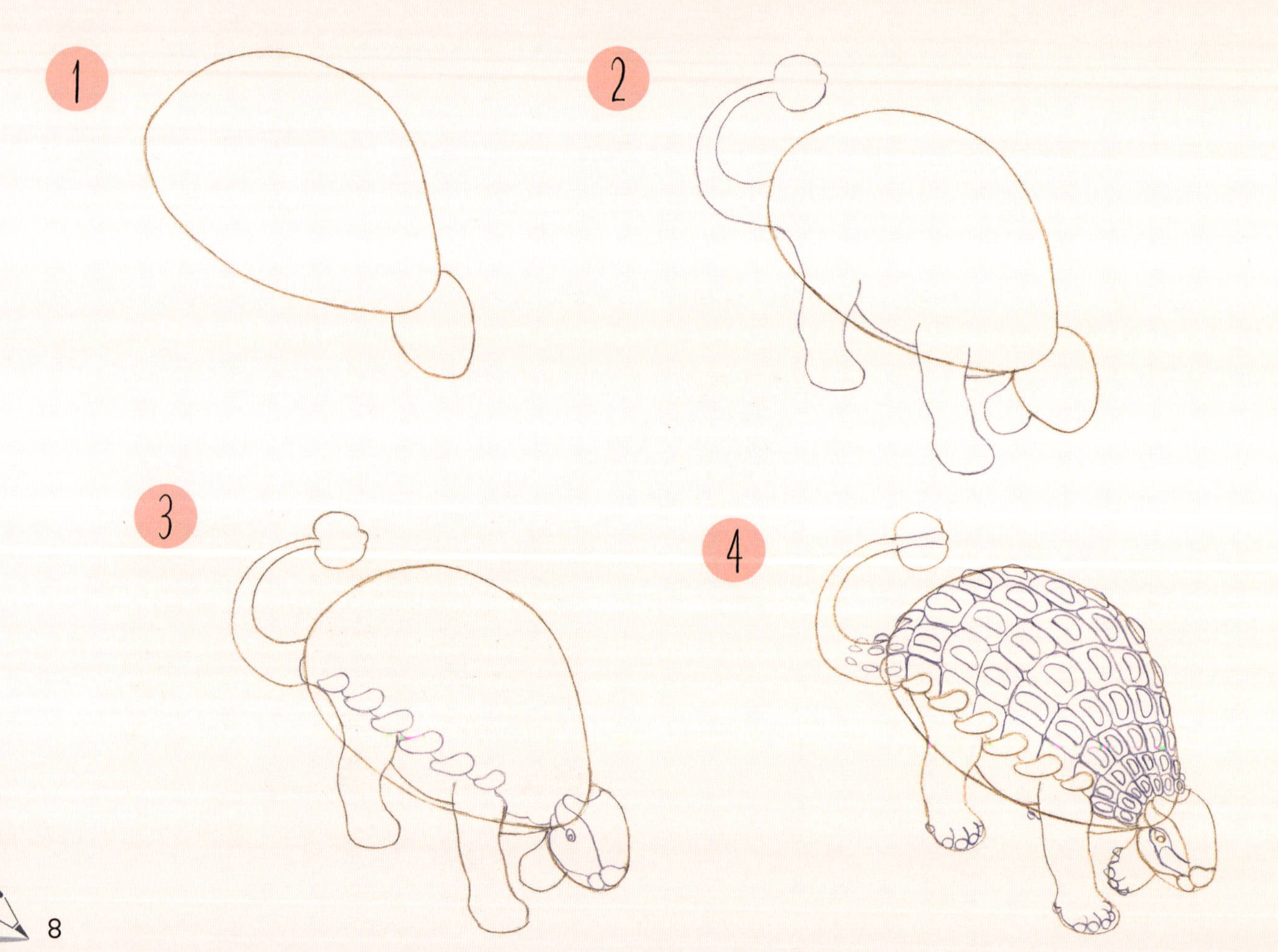
1
2
3
4

5

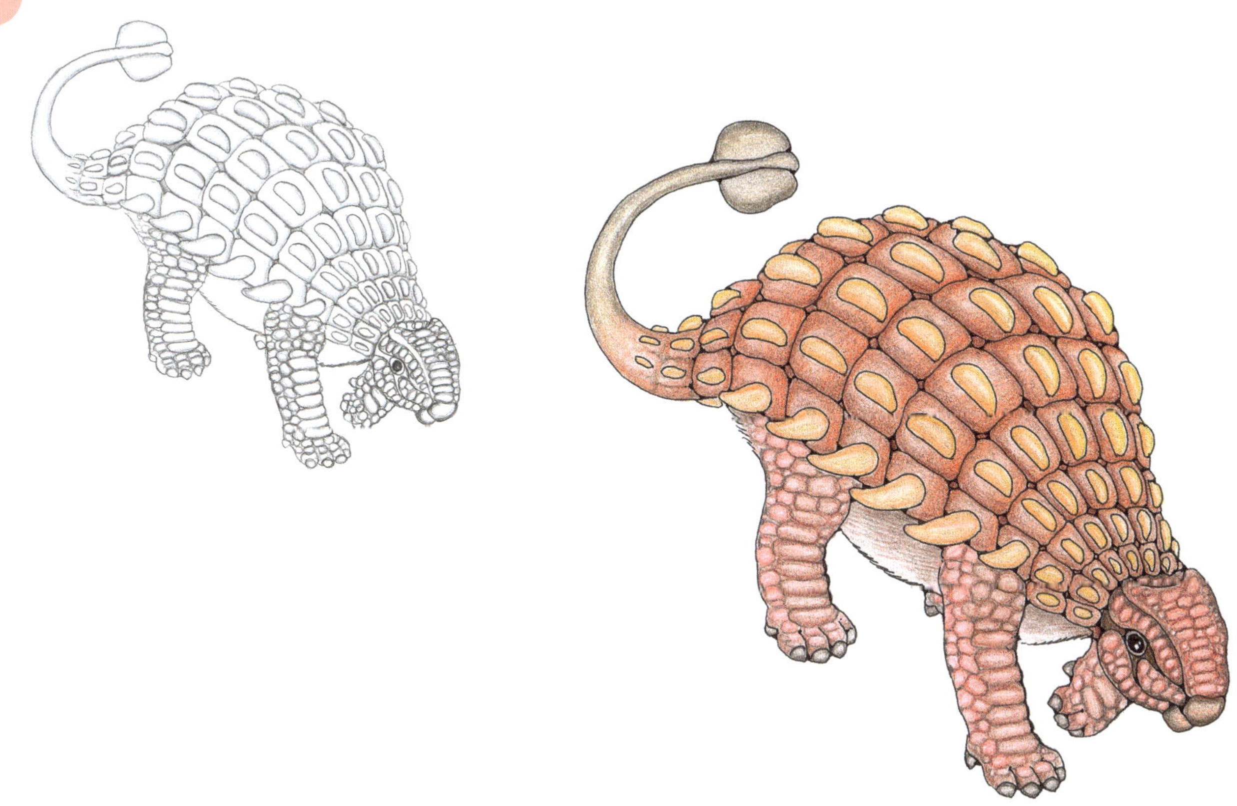

1

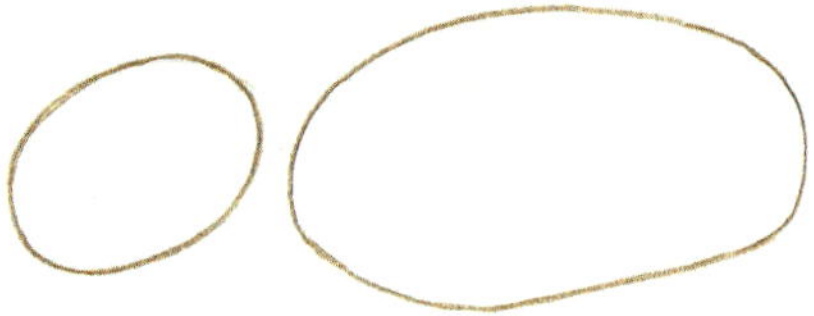

2

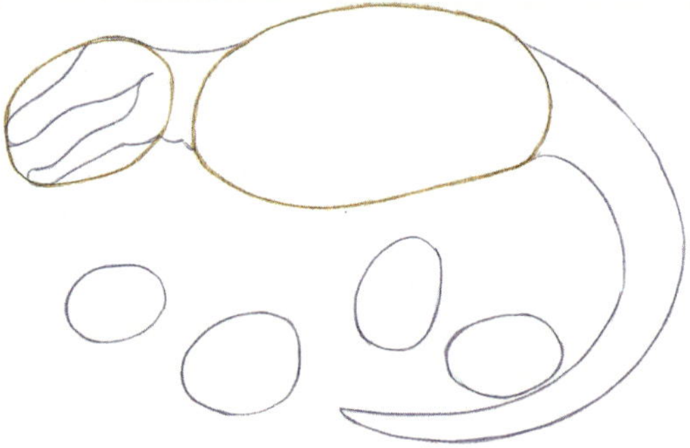

3

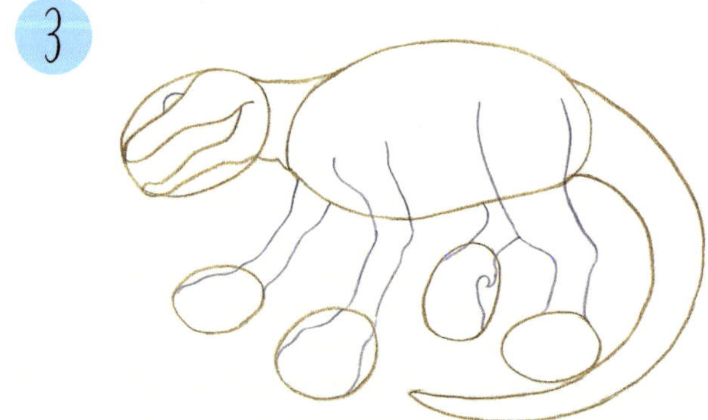

4

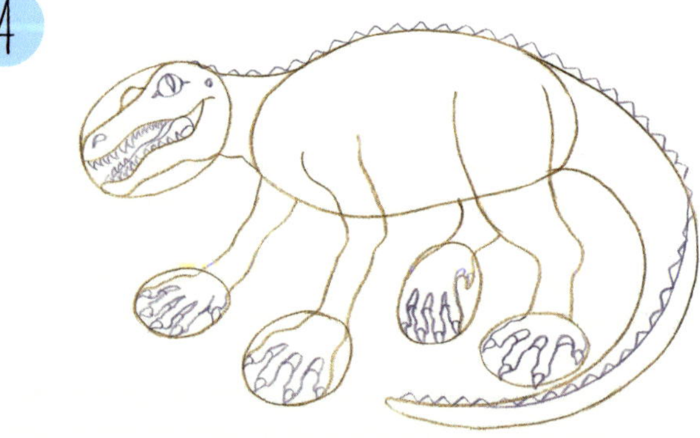

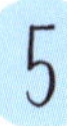
5

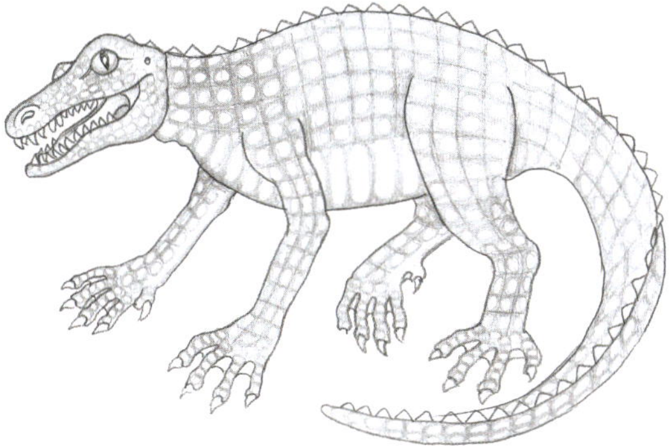

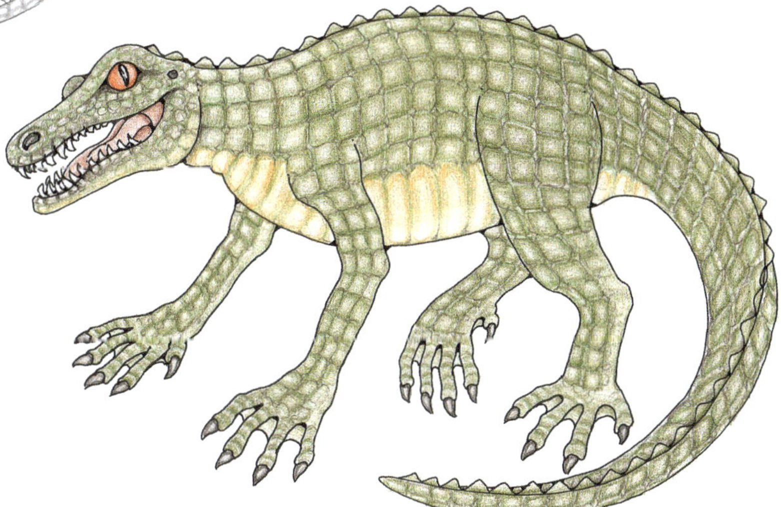

1

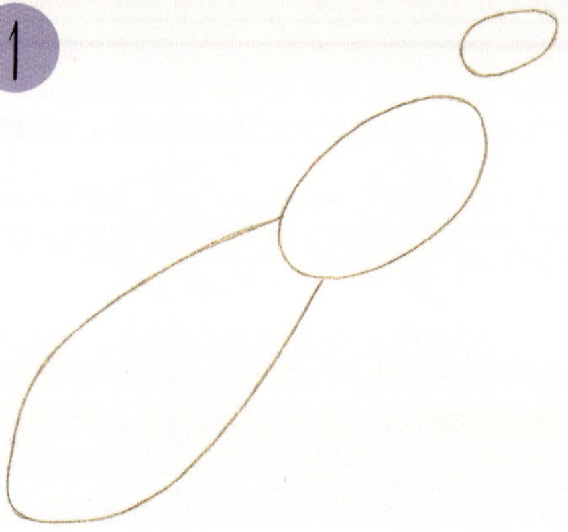

2

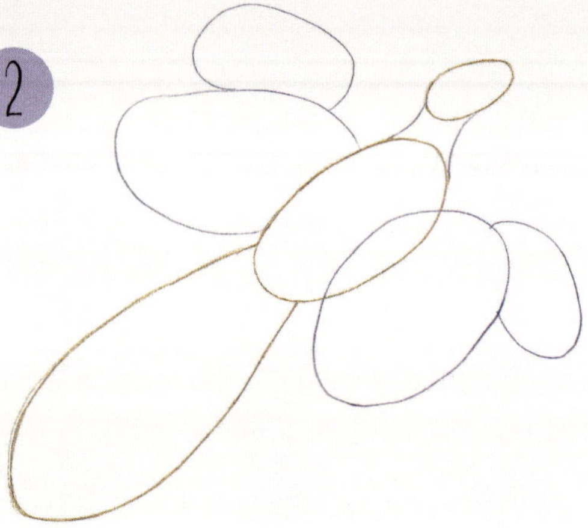

3

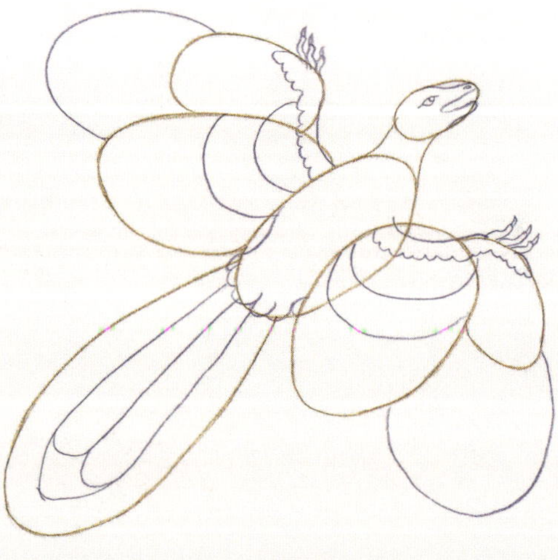

4

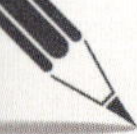

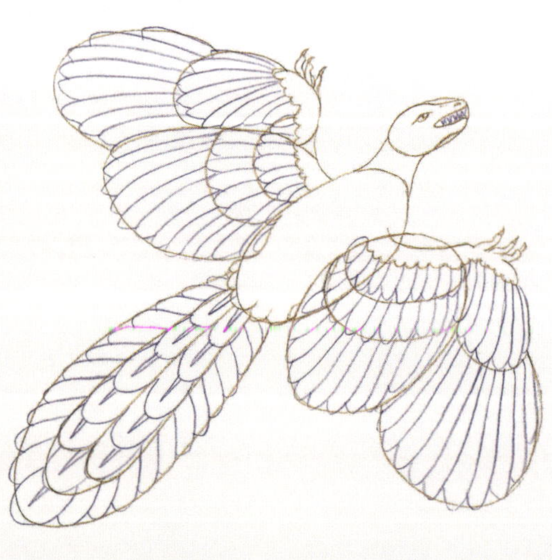

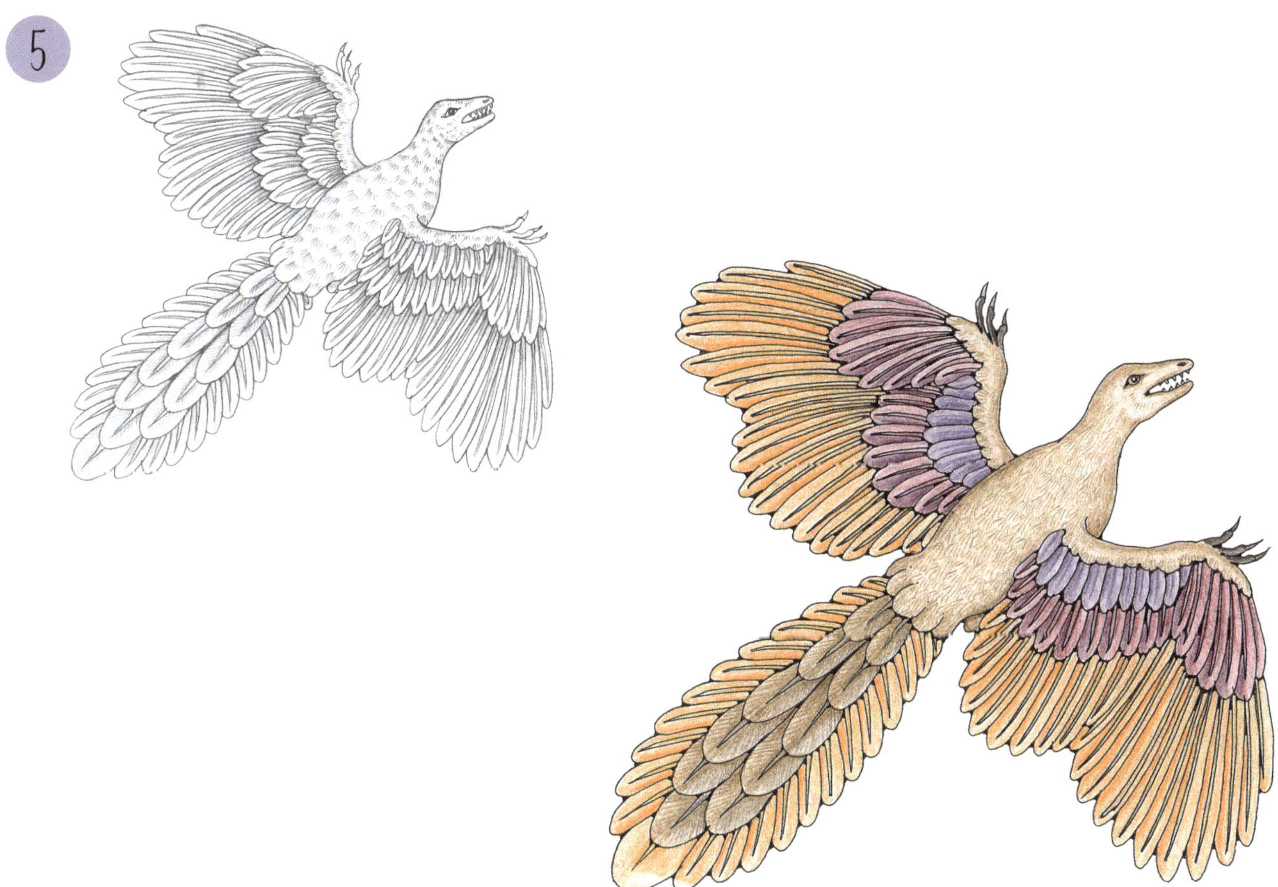
5

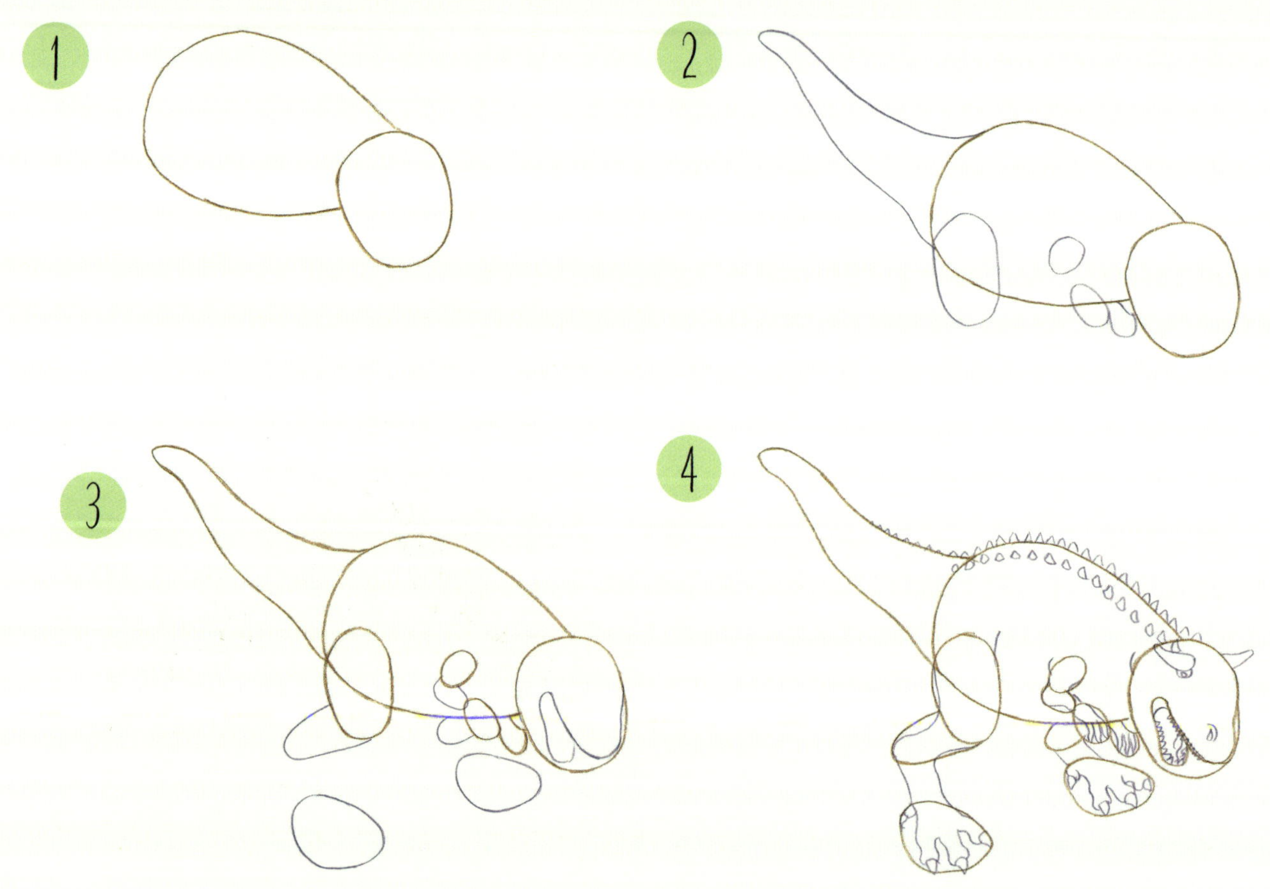
1
2
3
4

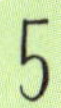
5

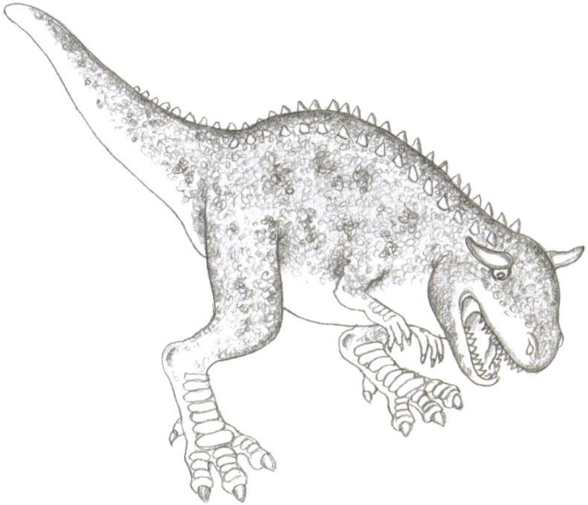

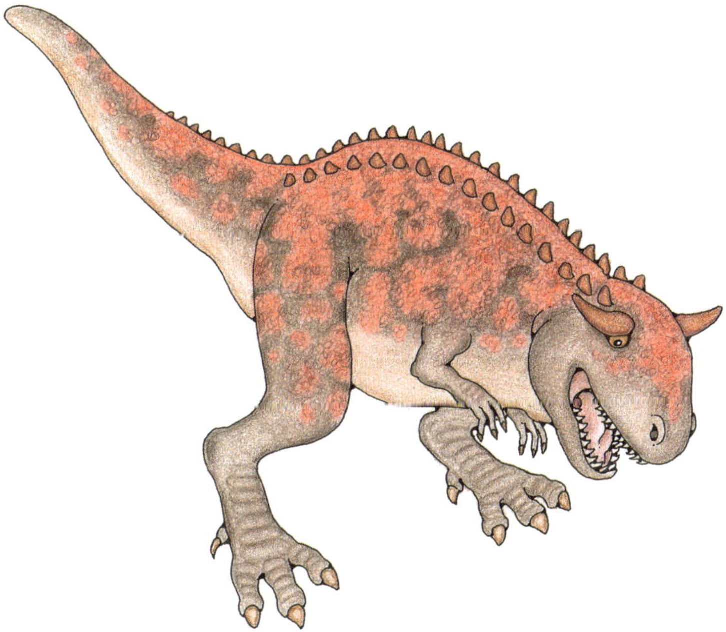

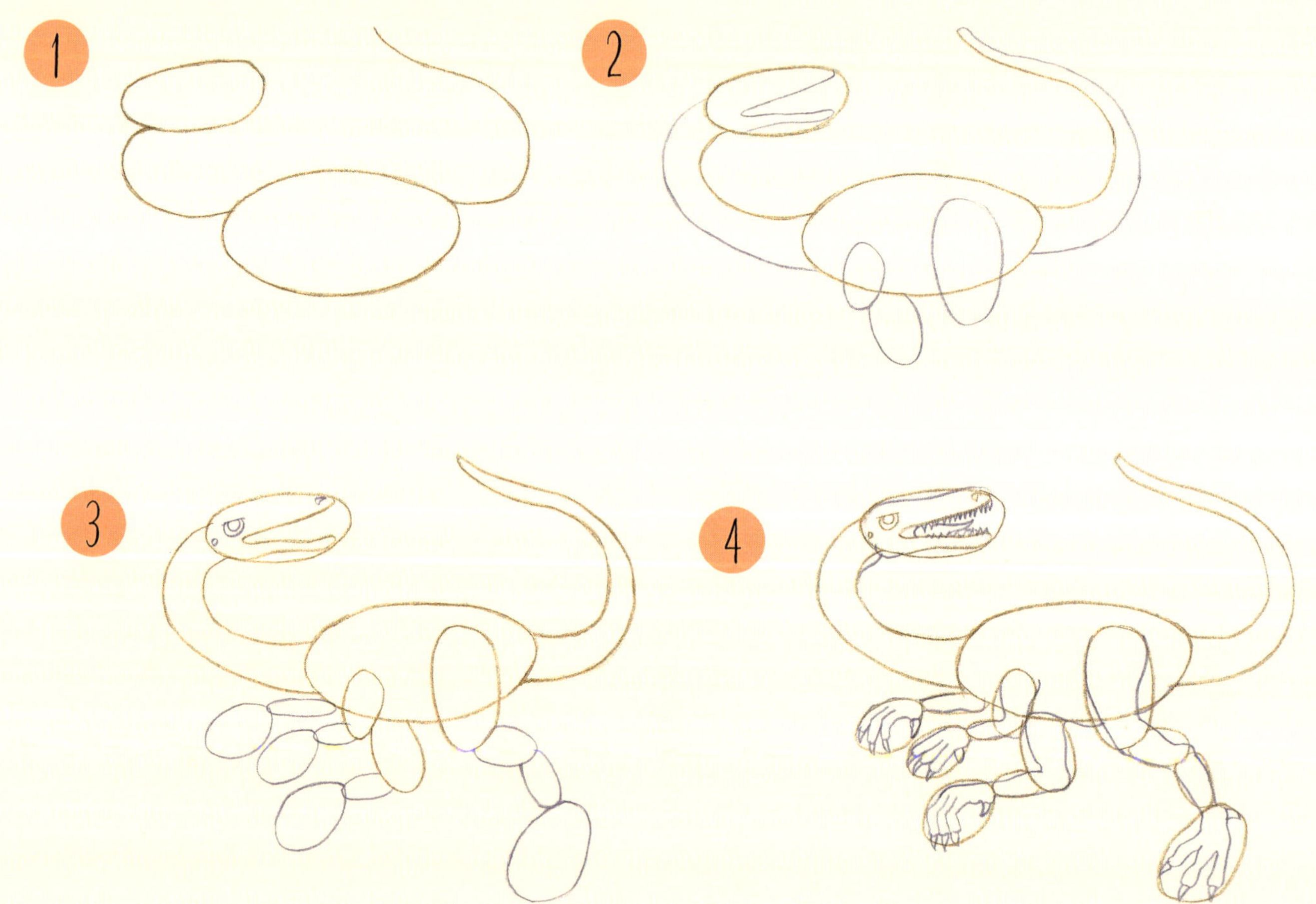
1
2
3
4

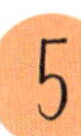

5

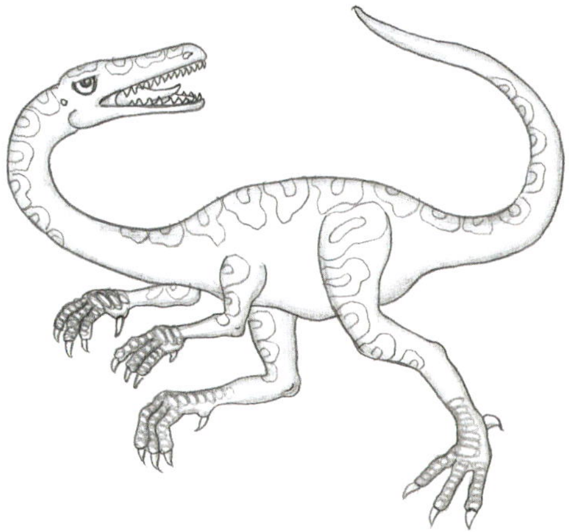

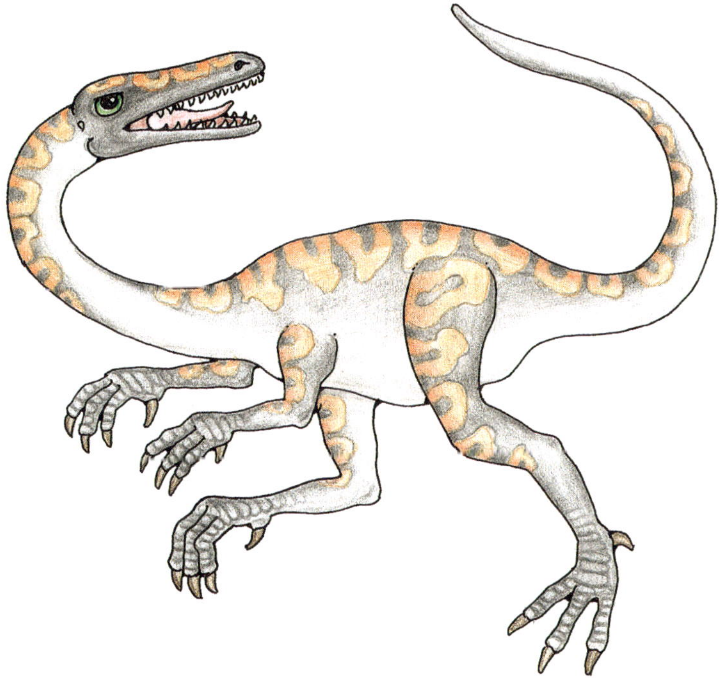

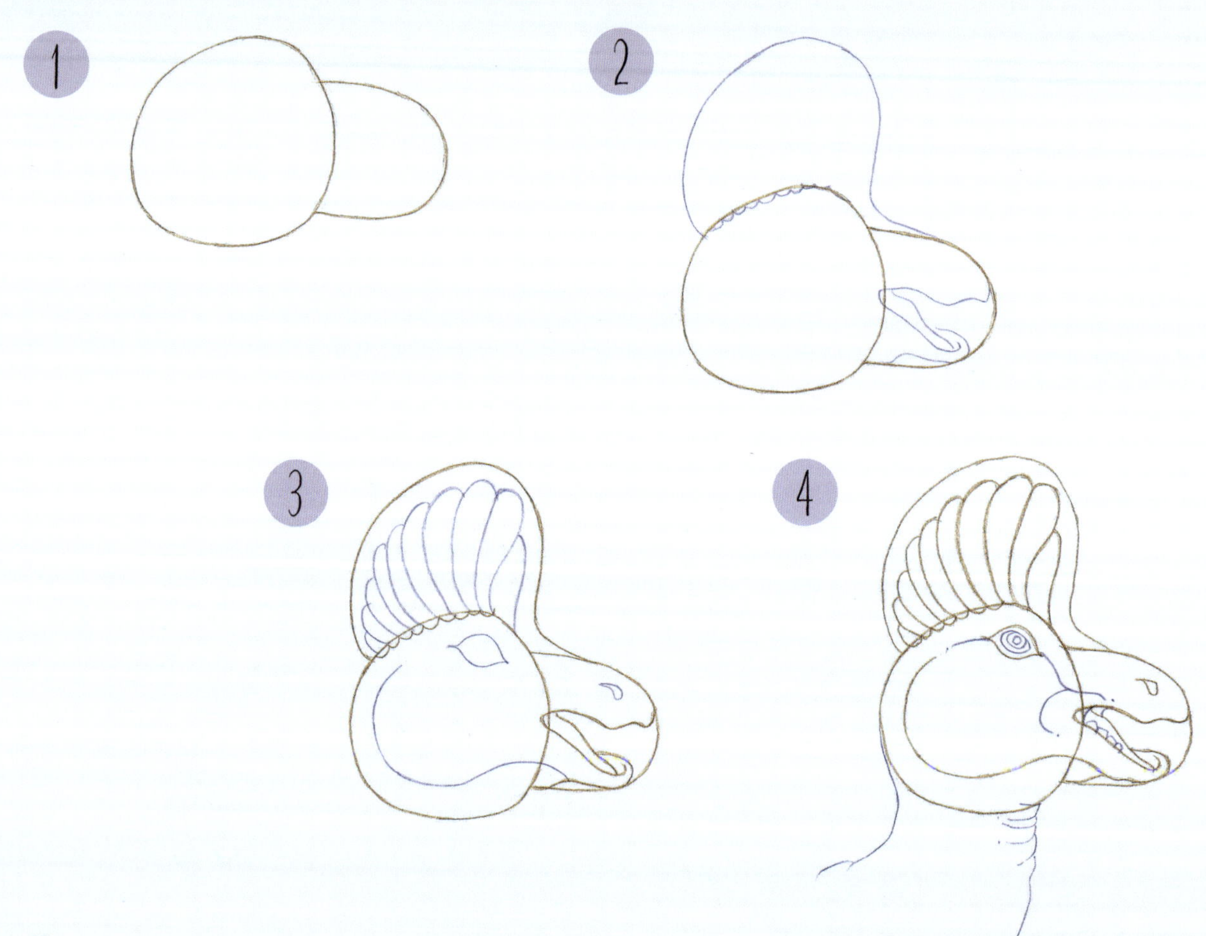
1
2
3
4

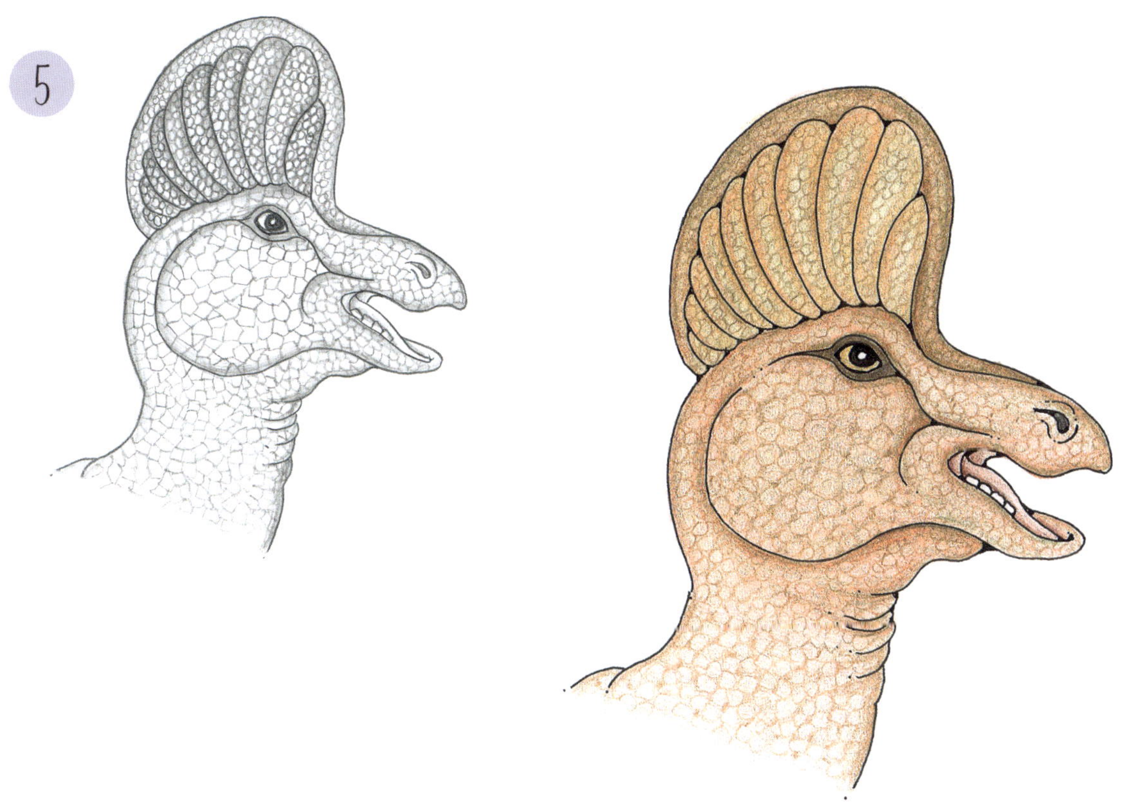
5

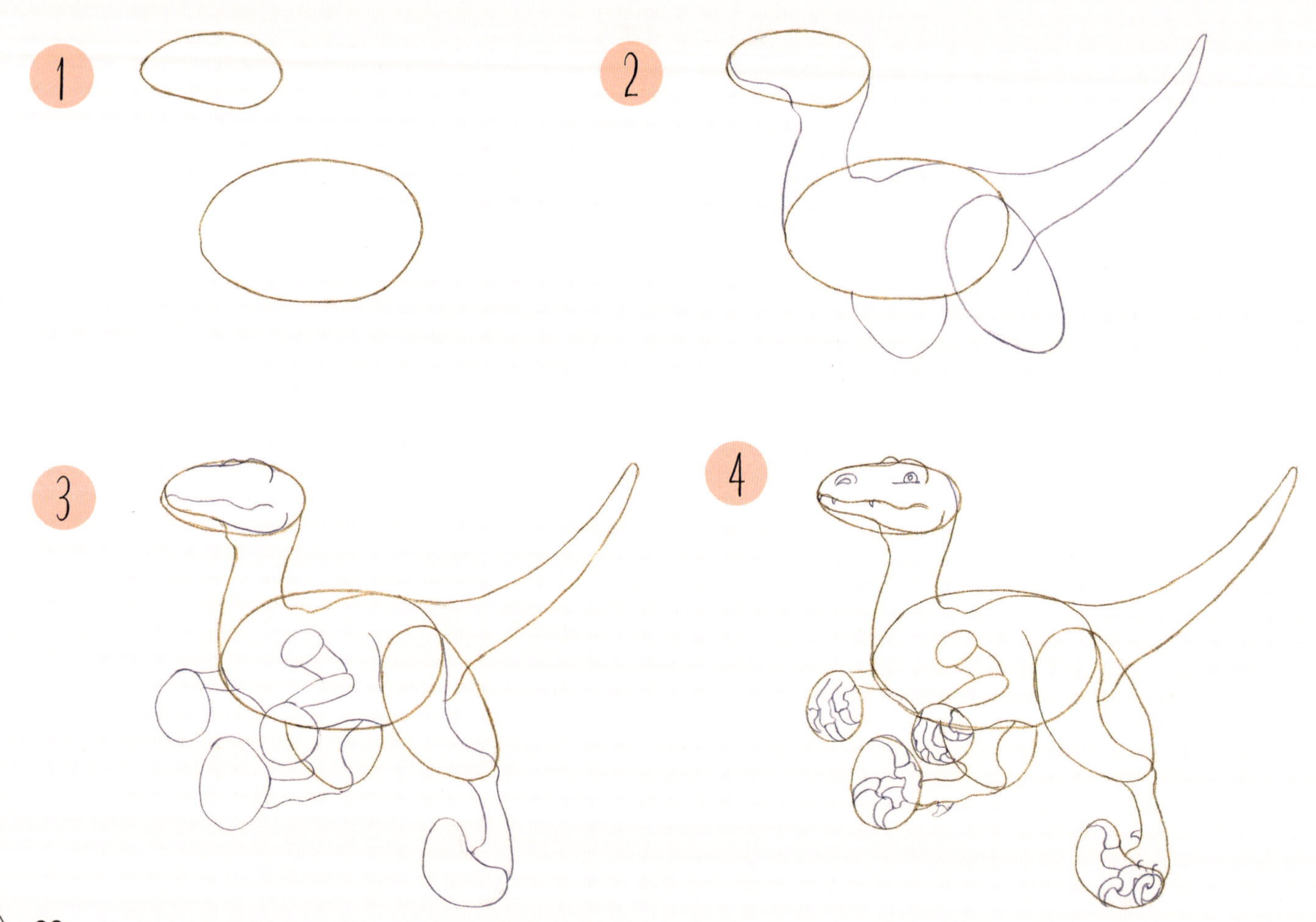

1
2
3
4

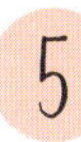
5

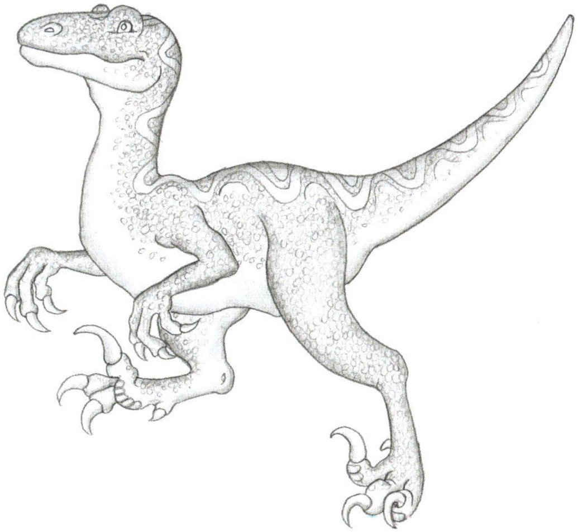

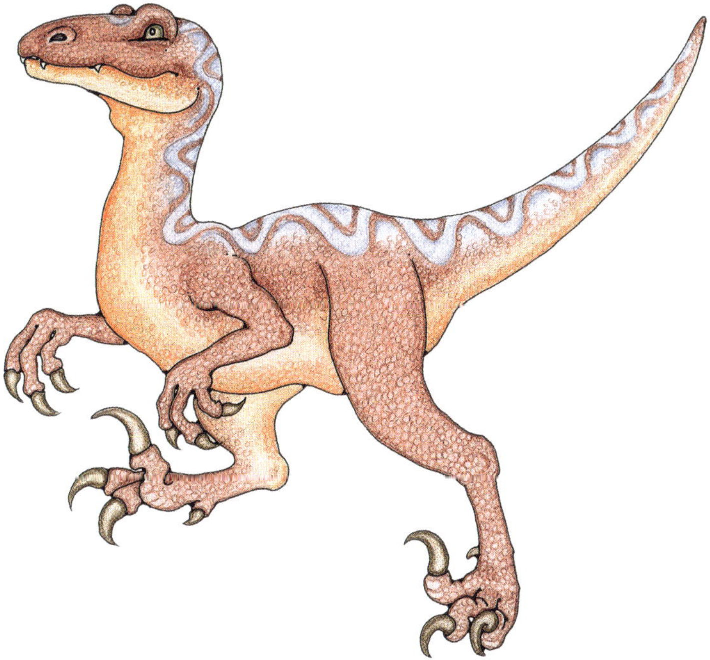

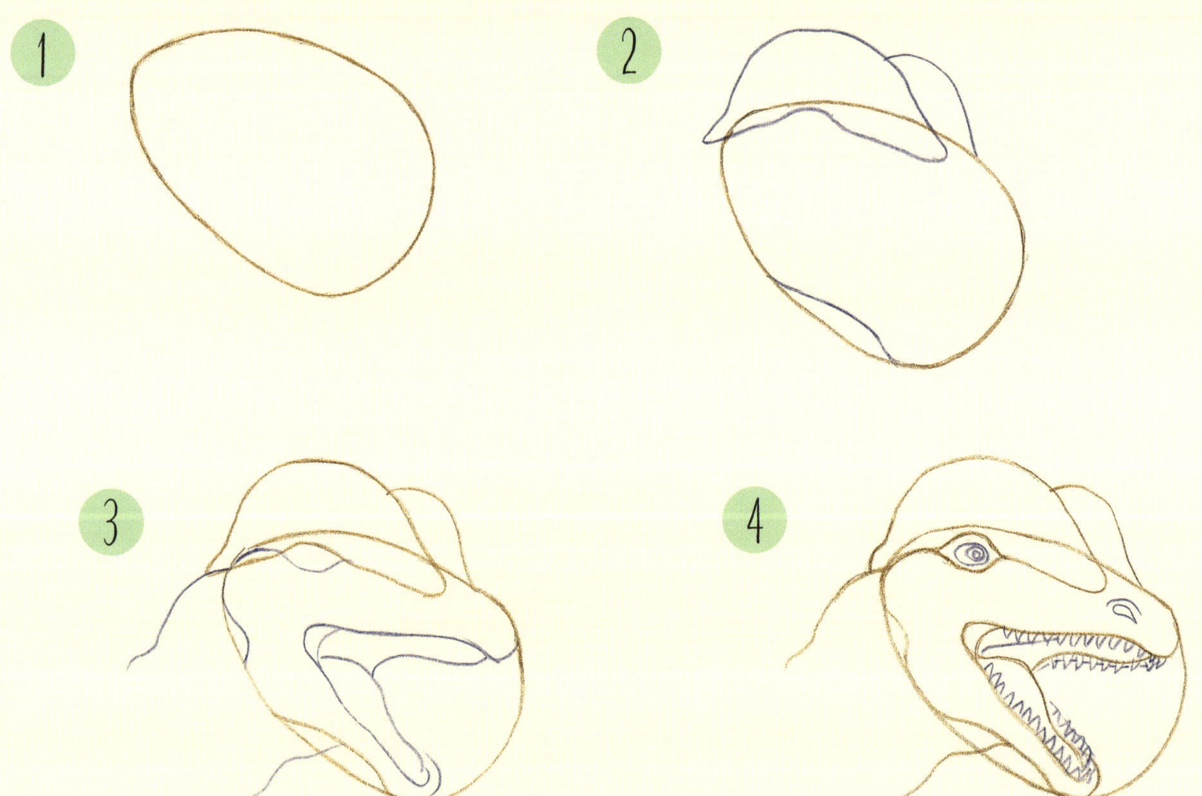
1
2
3
4

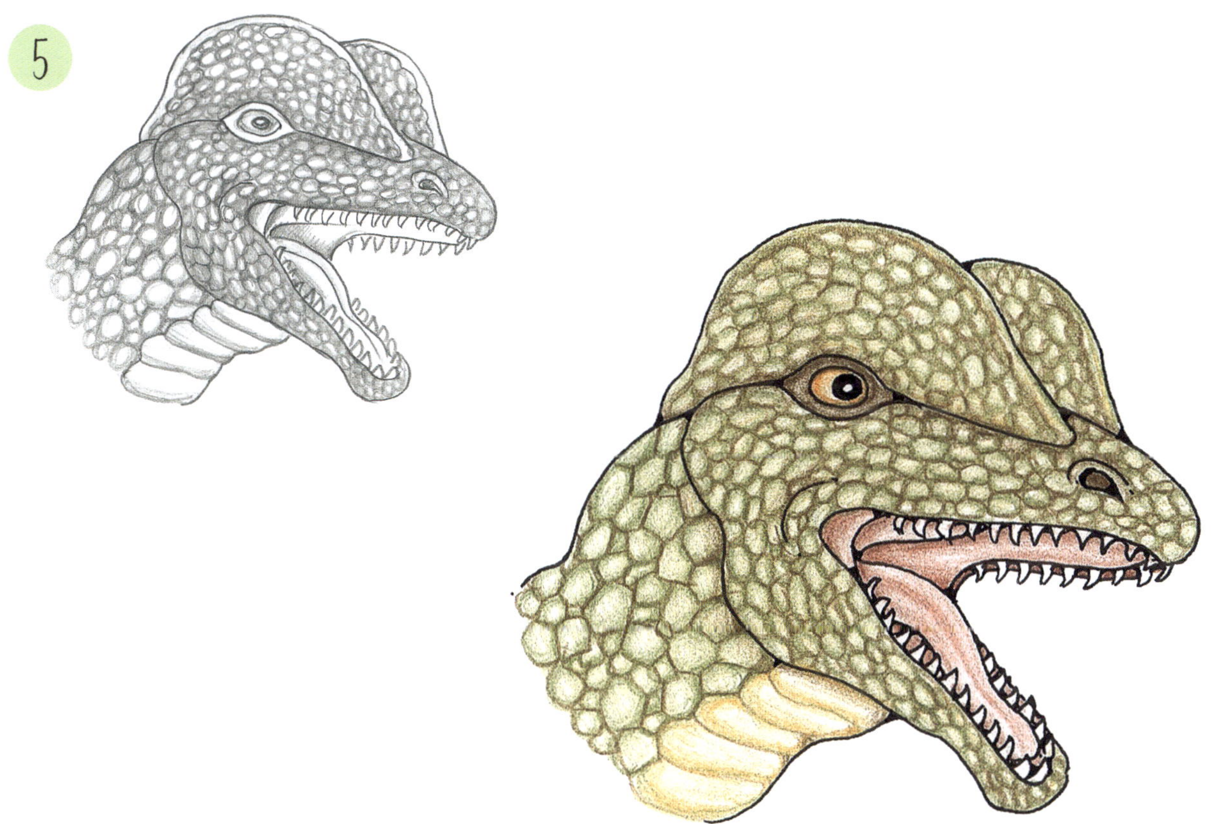
5

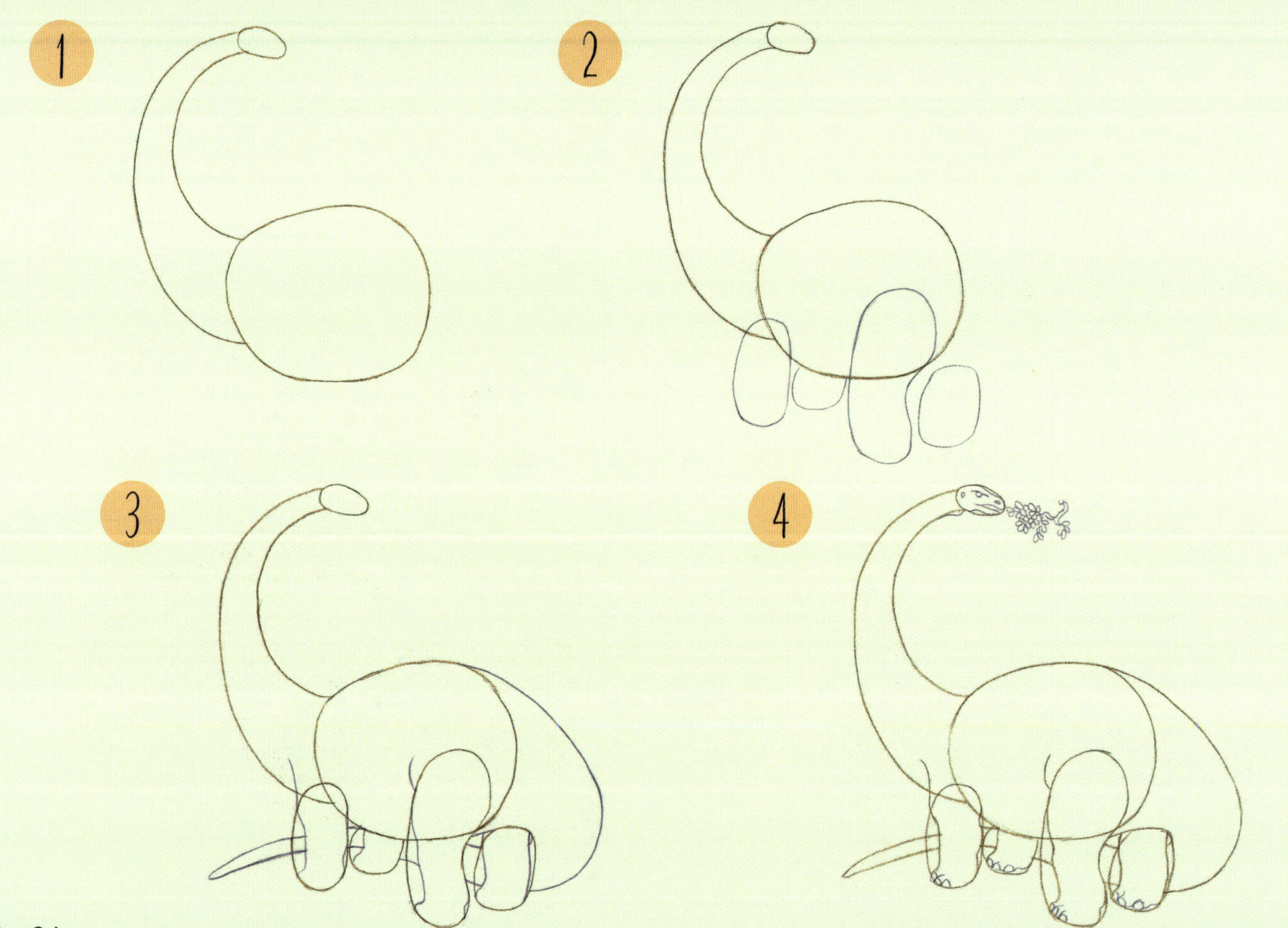
1
2
3
4

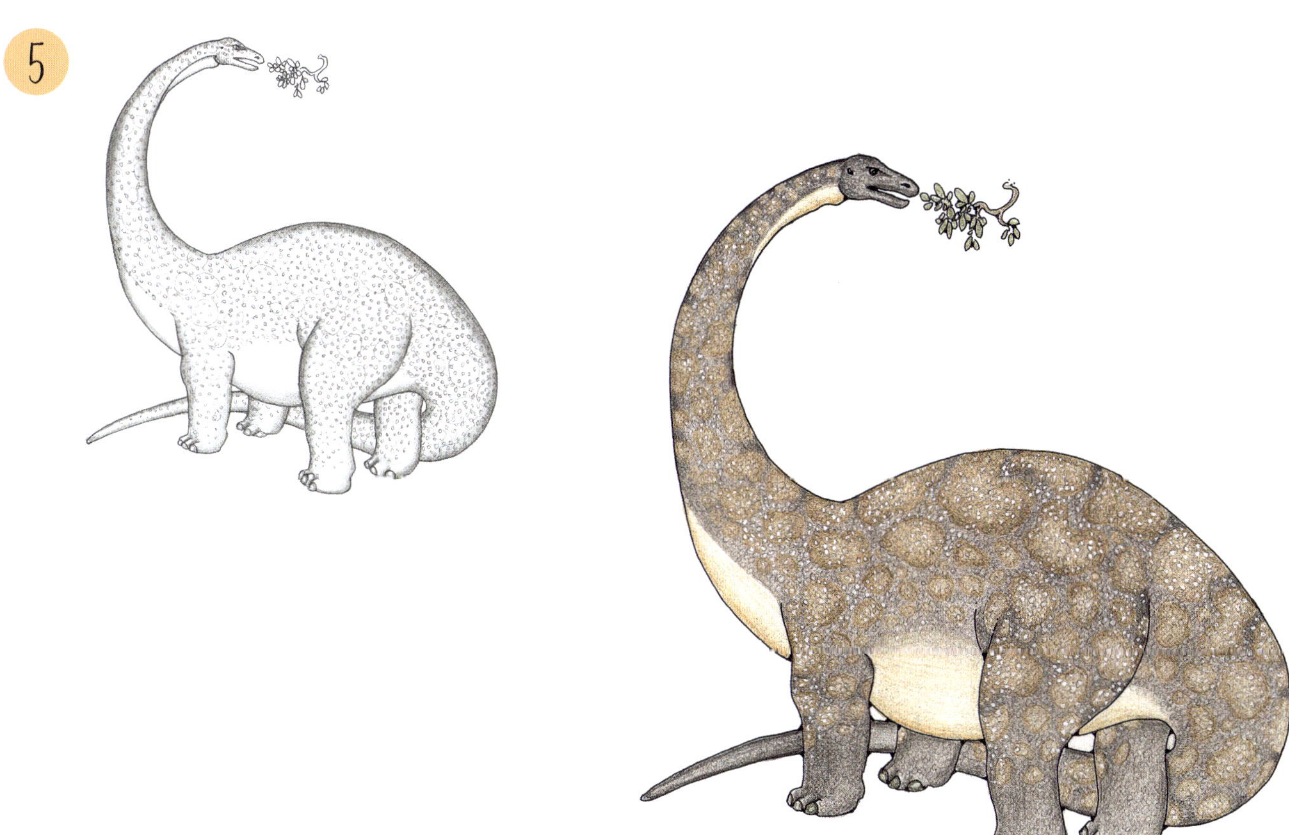
5

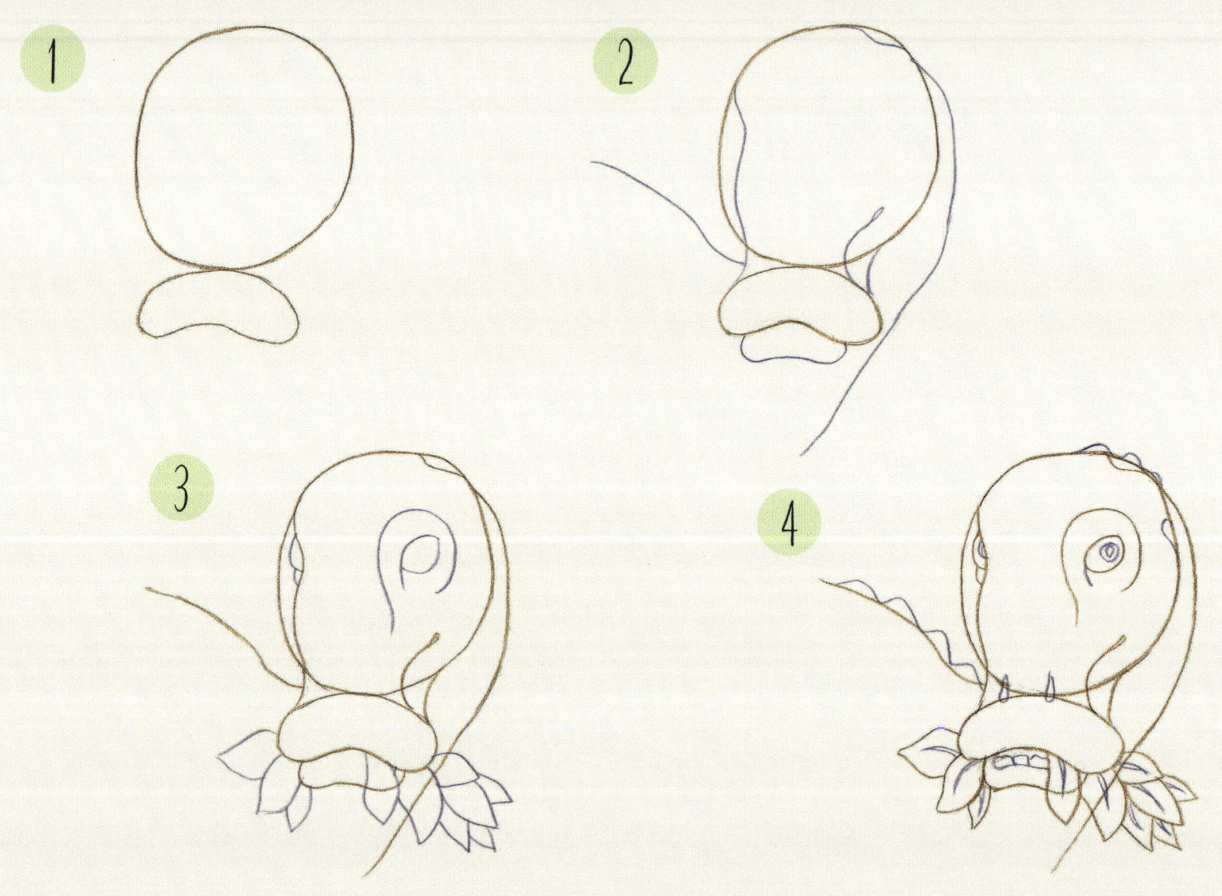
1
2
3
4

5

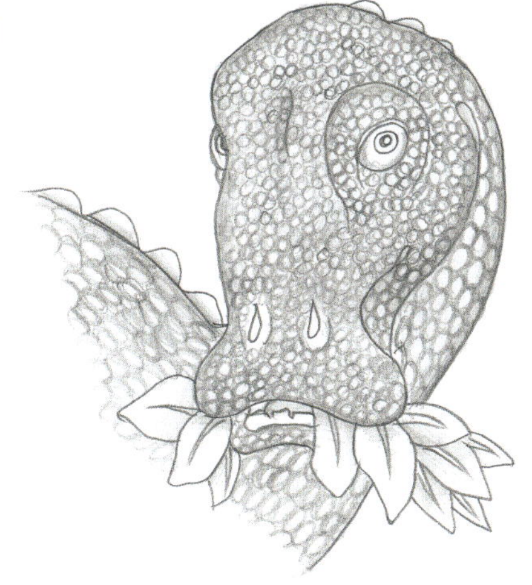

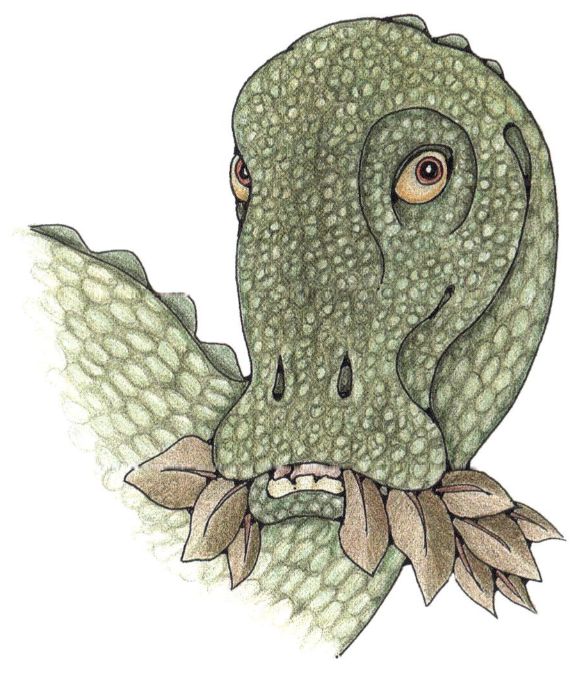

1

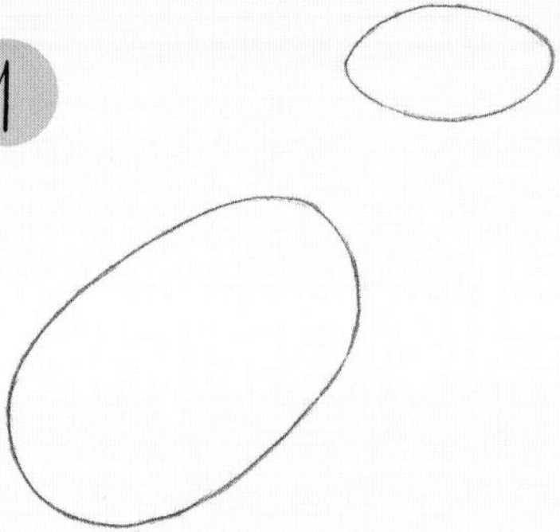

2

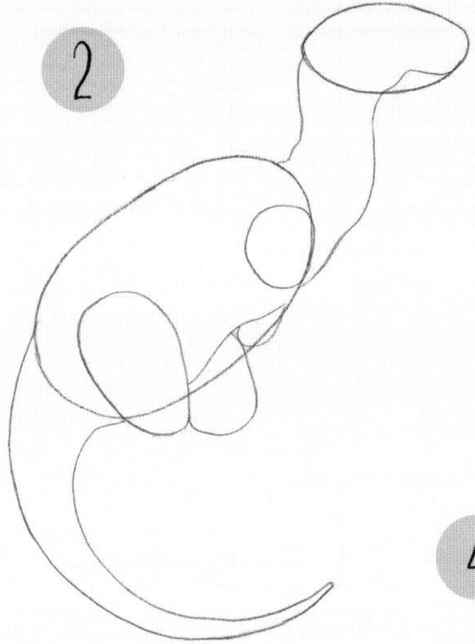

3

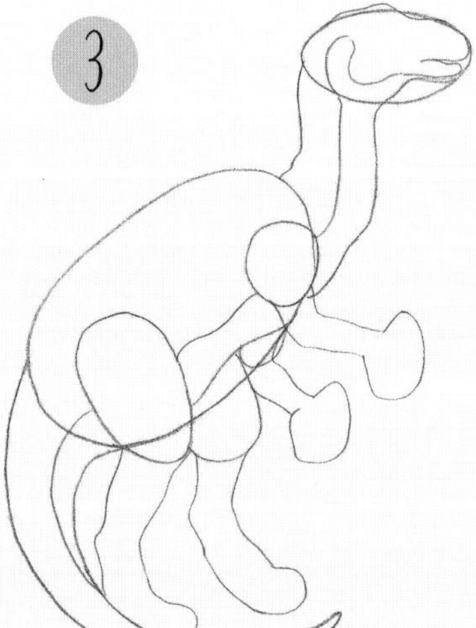

4

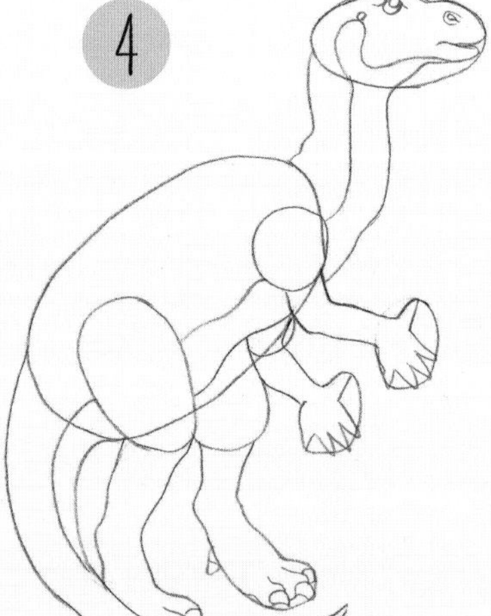

5

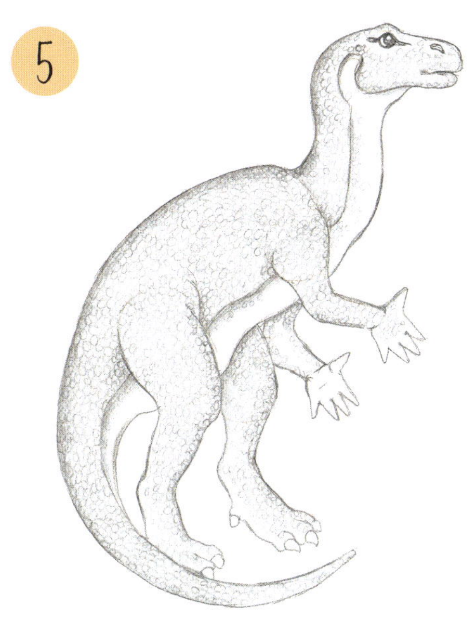

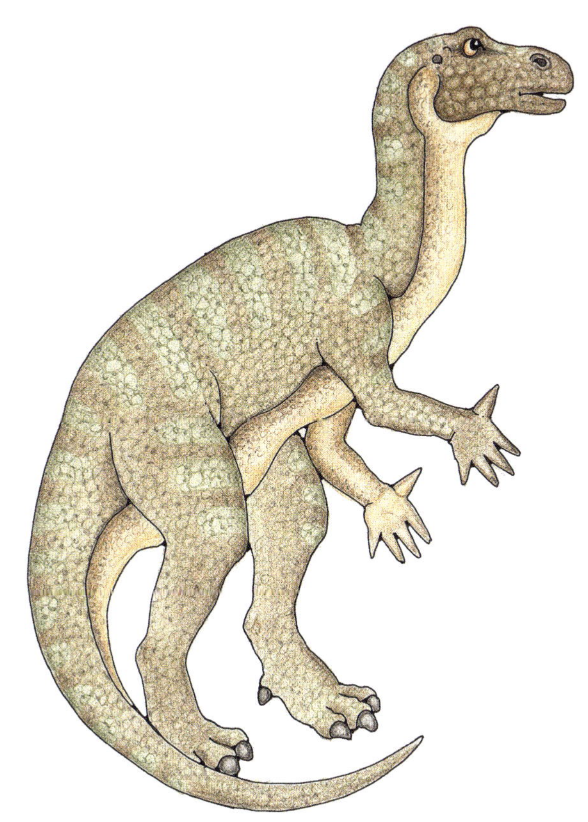

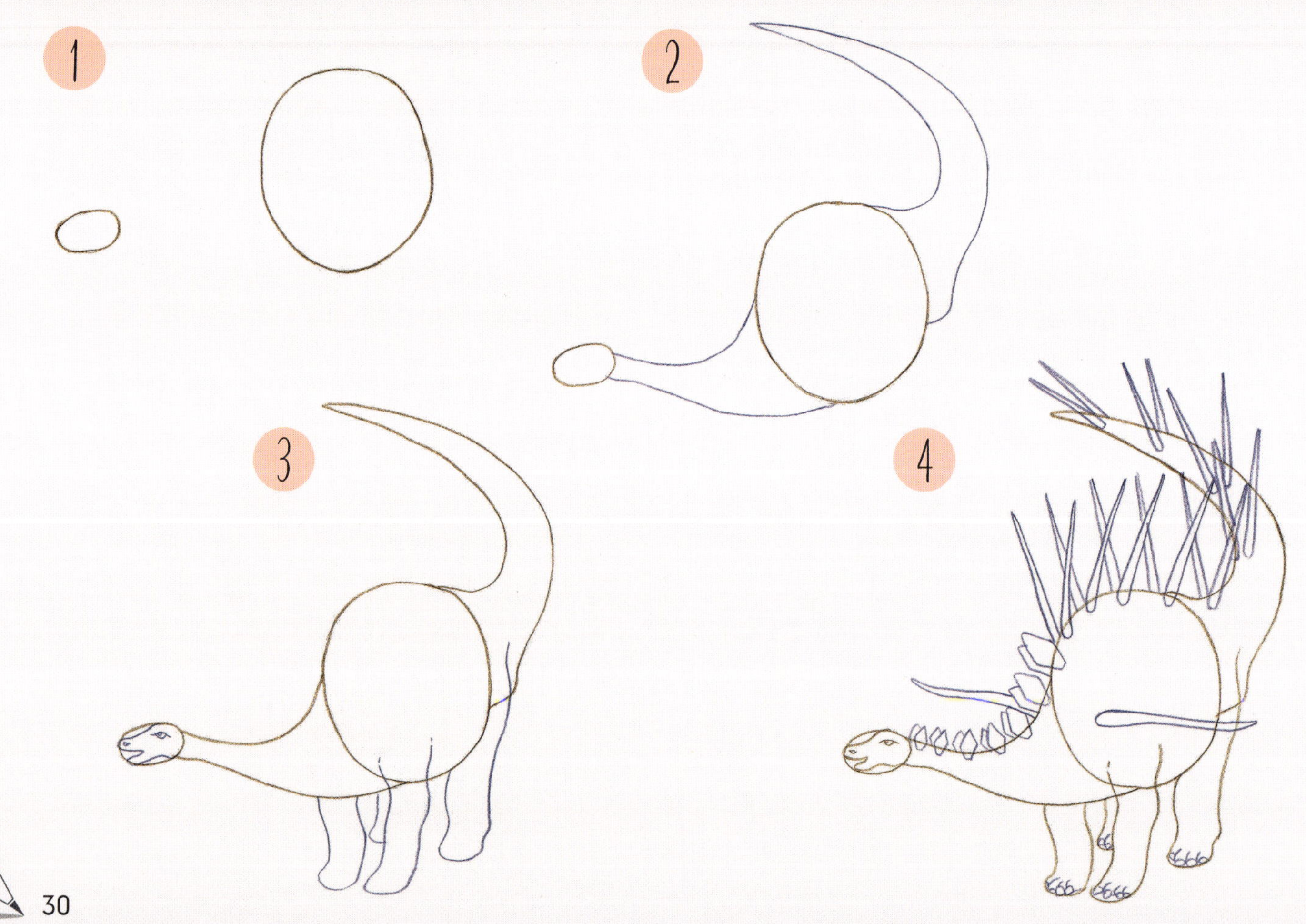
1
2
3
4

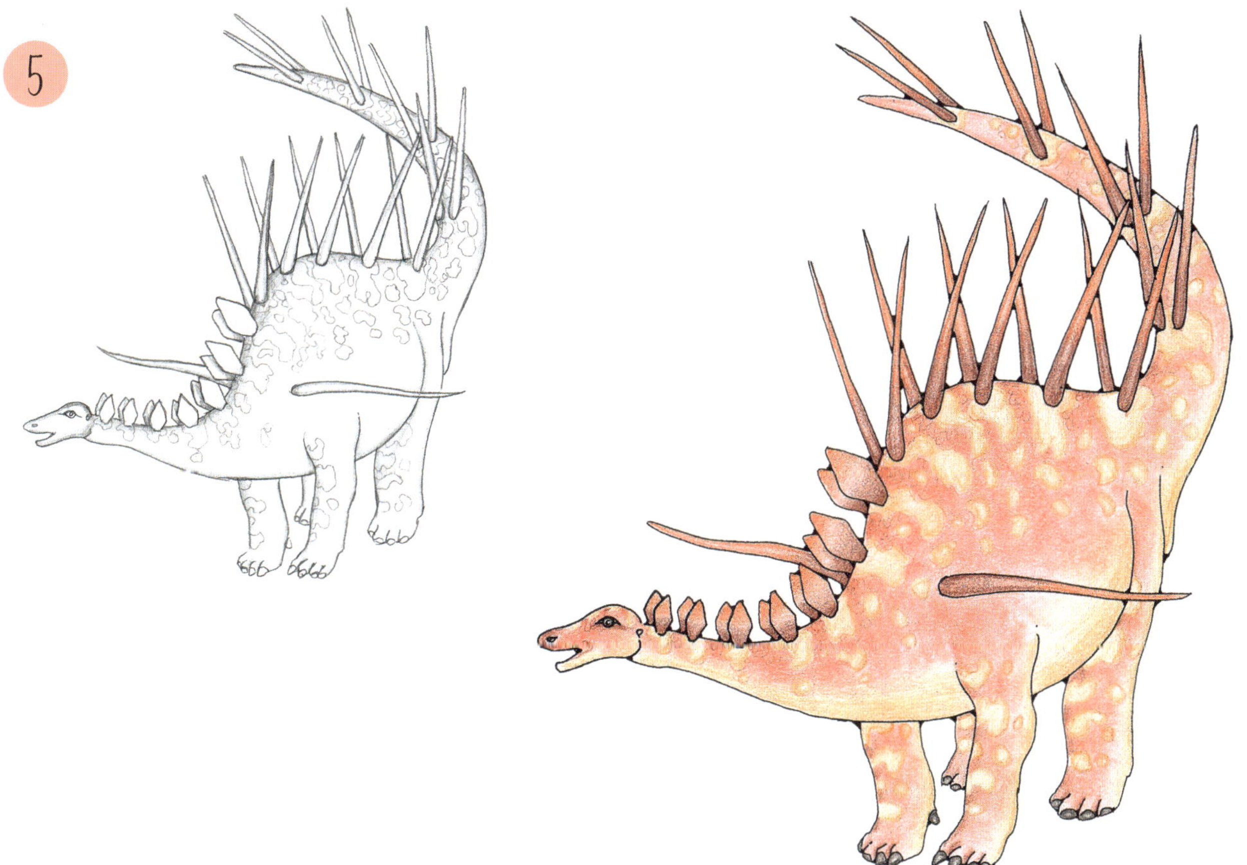
5

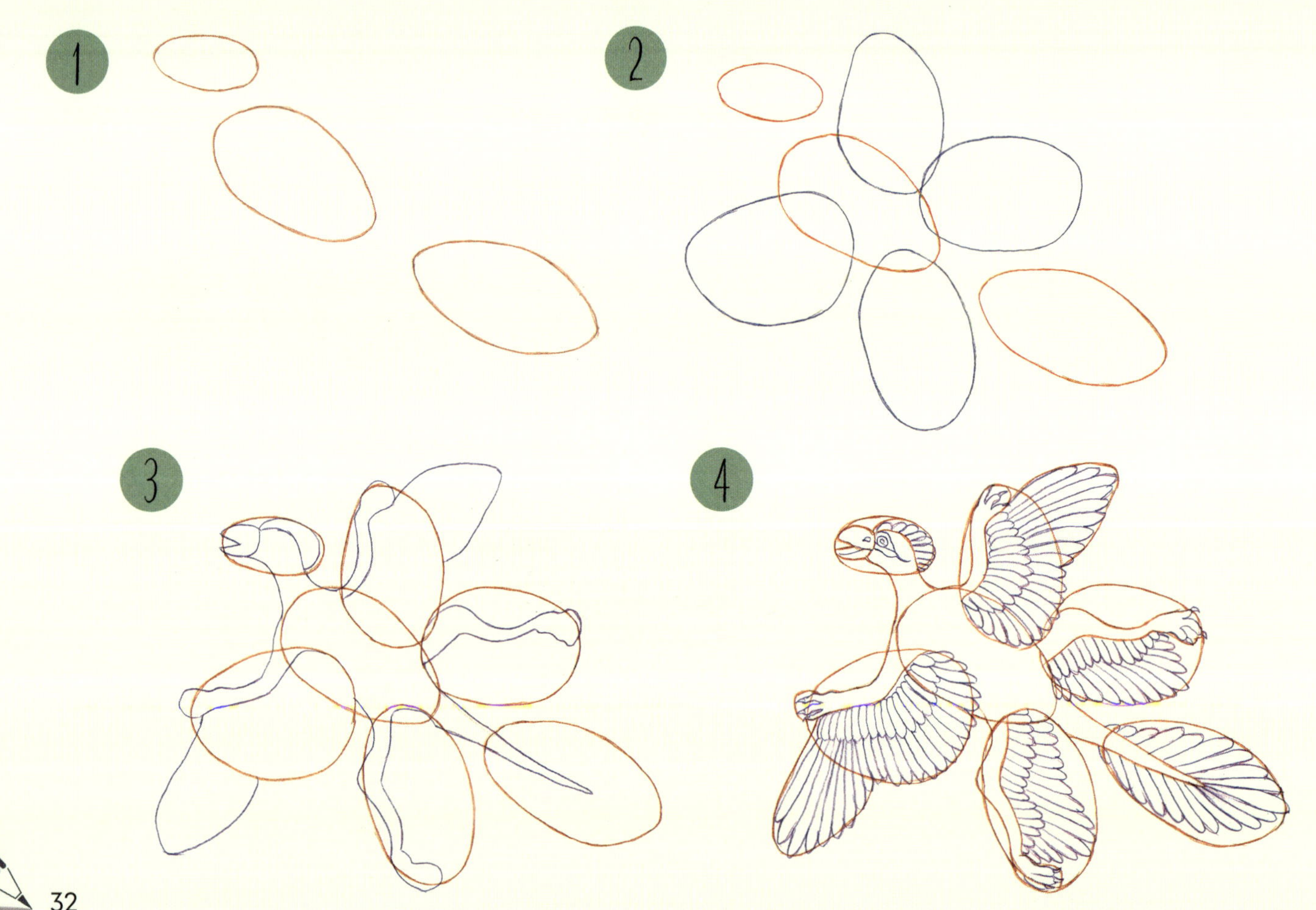
1
2
3
4

5

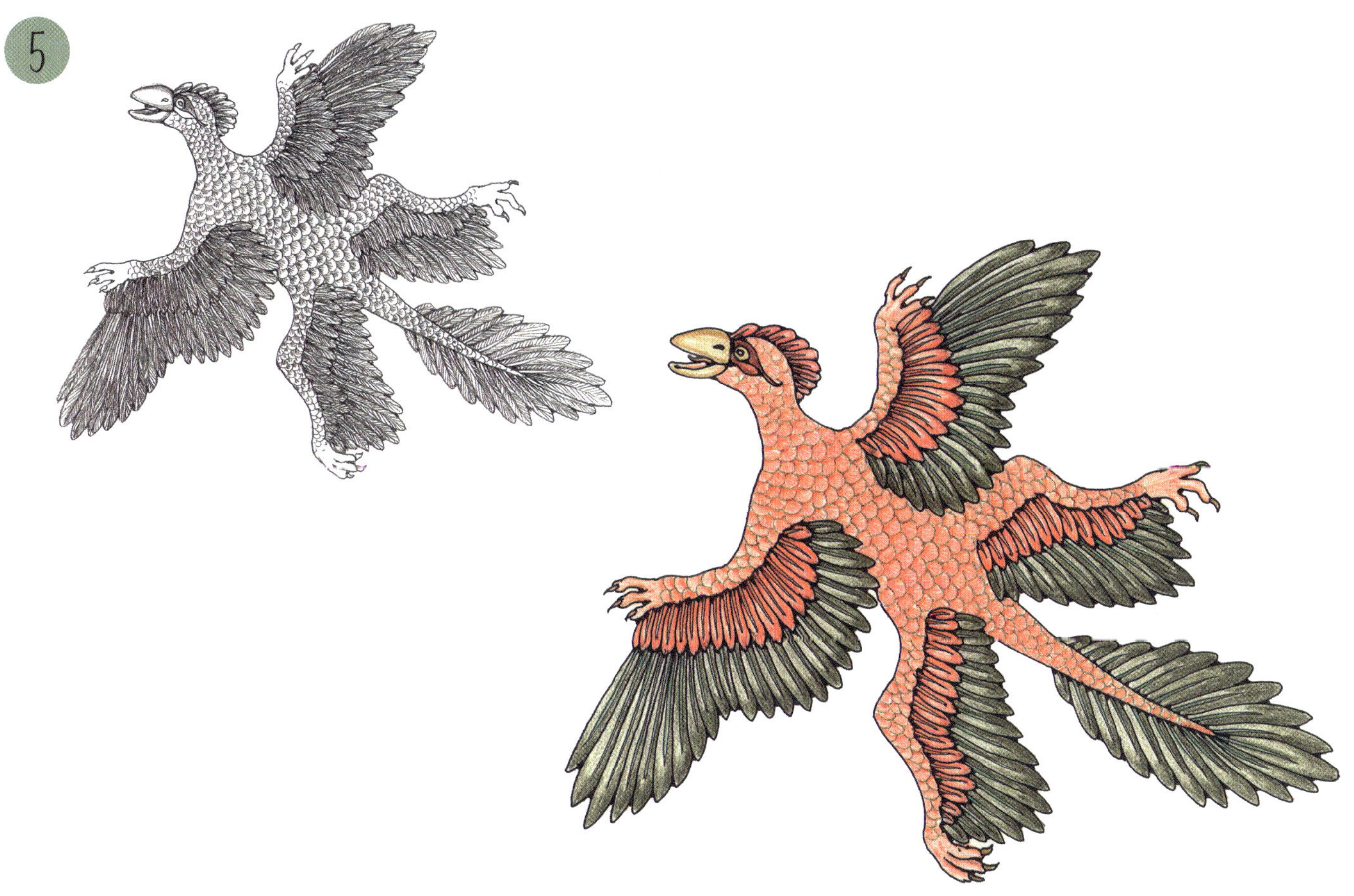

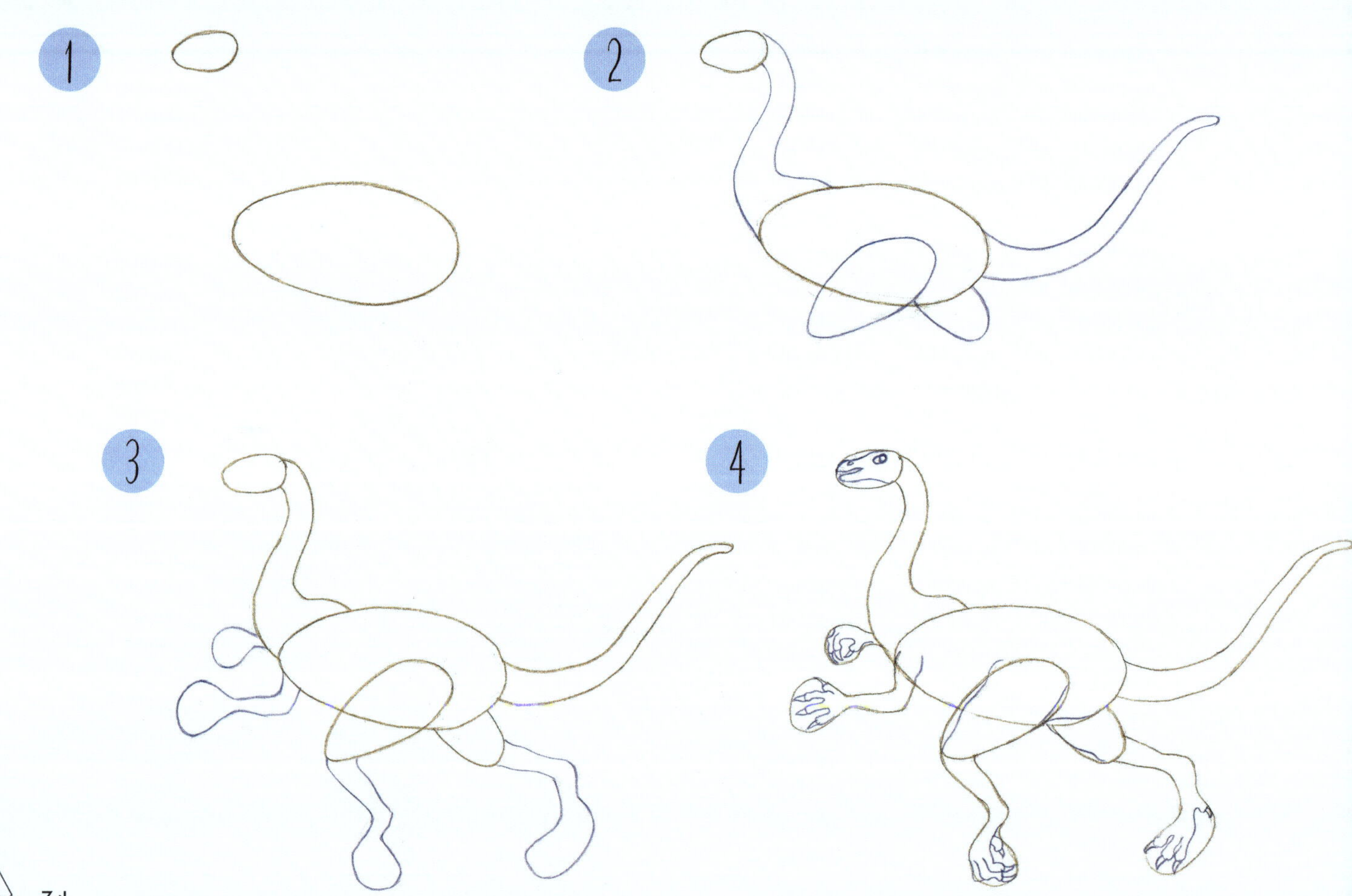
1
2
3
4

5

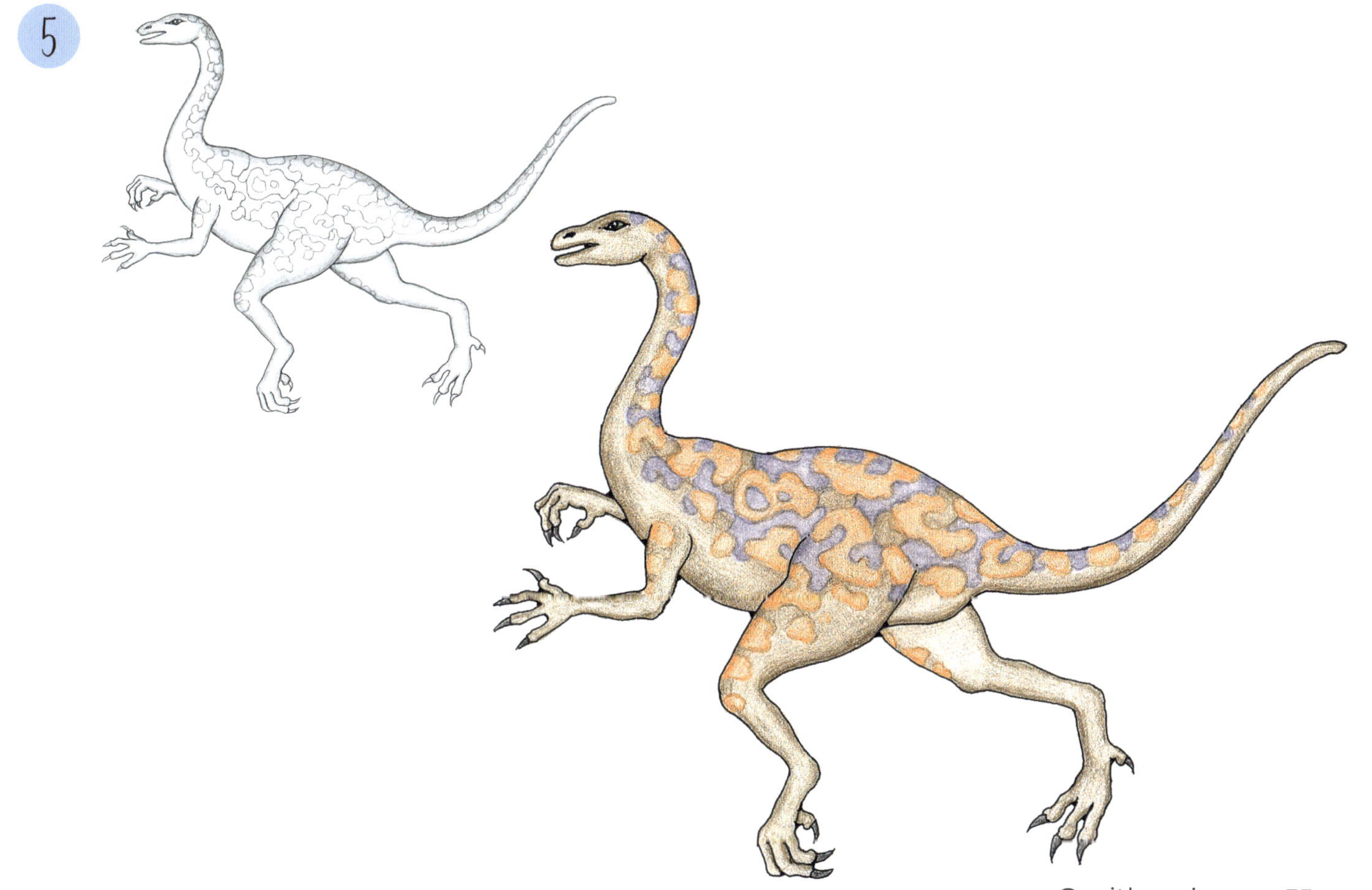

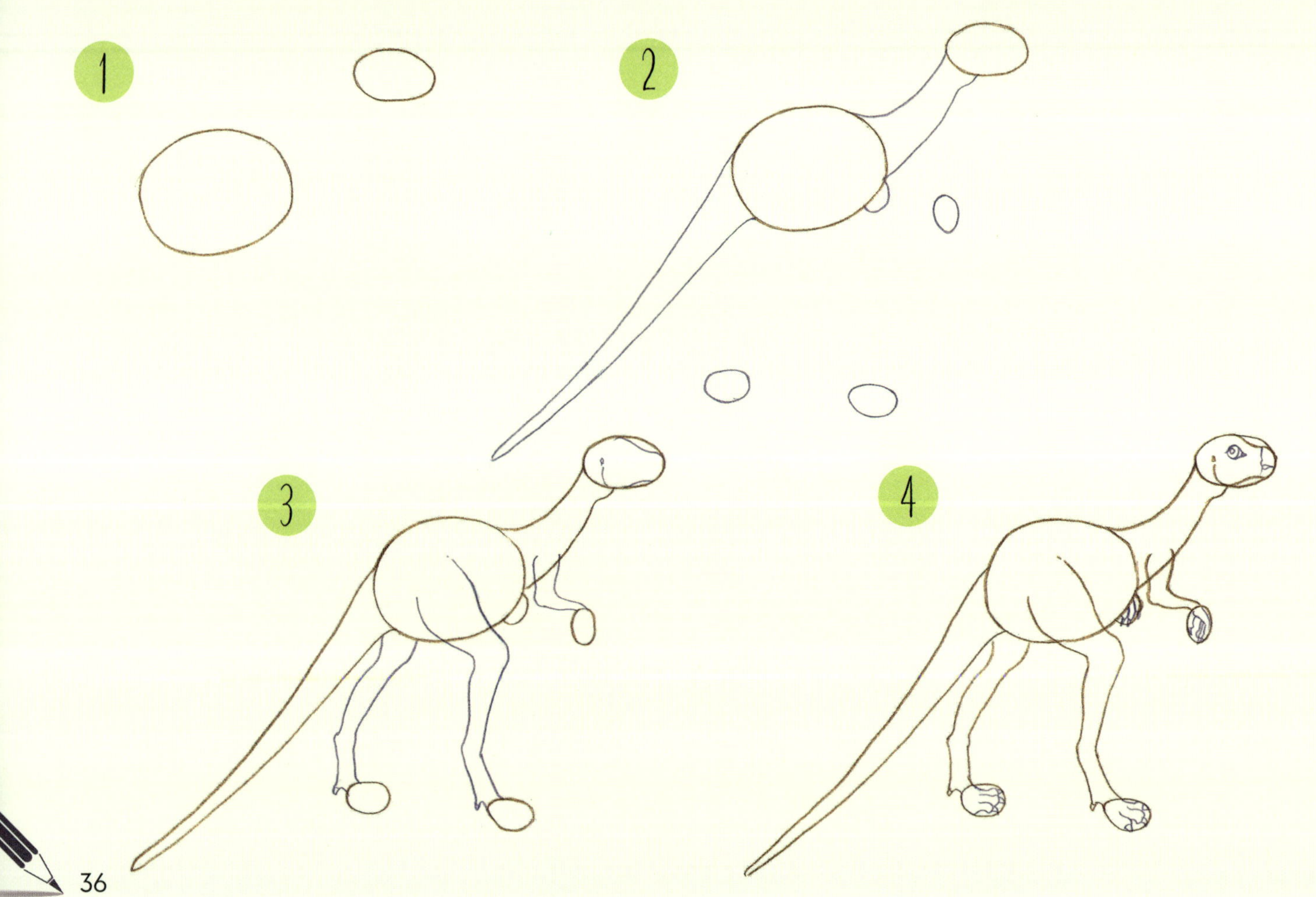

1
2
3
4

5

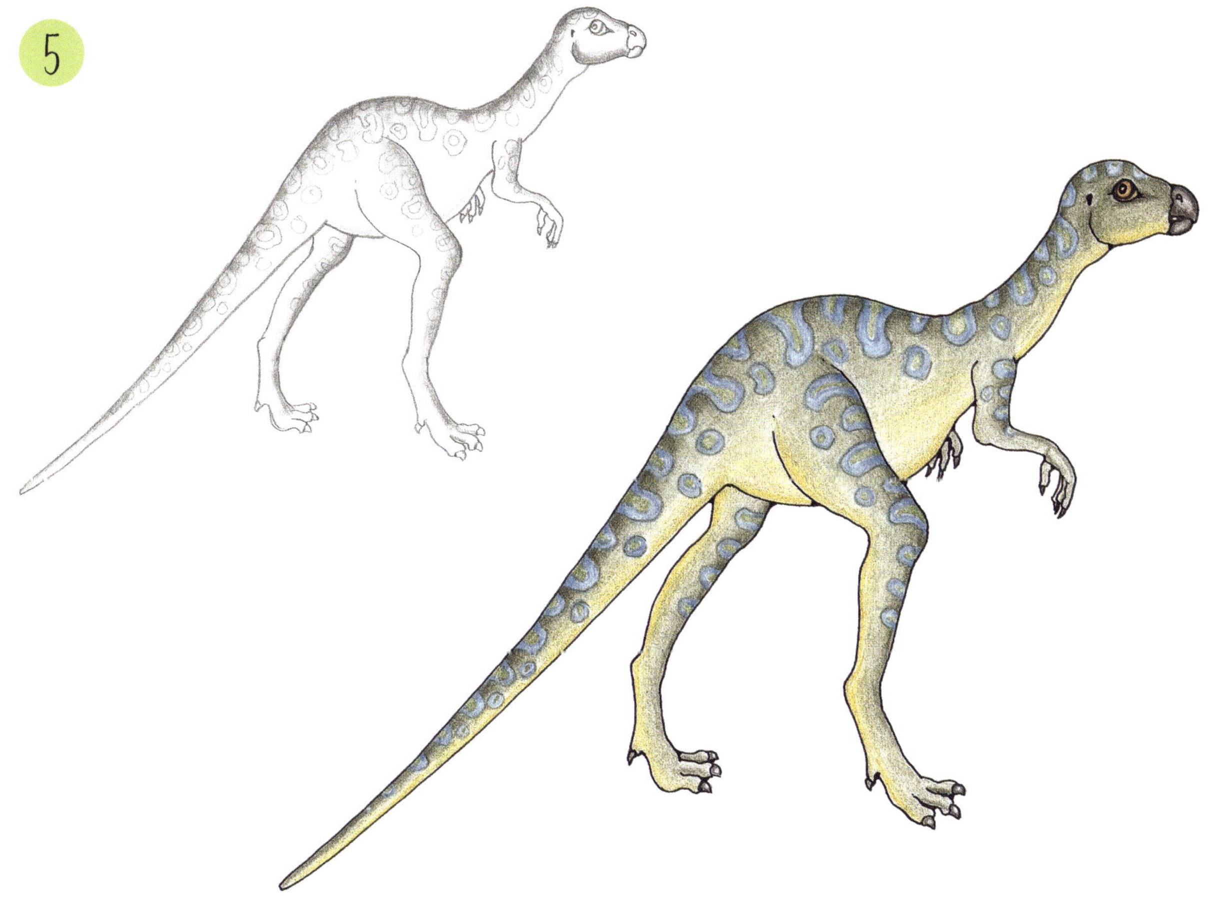

1

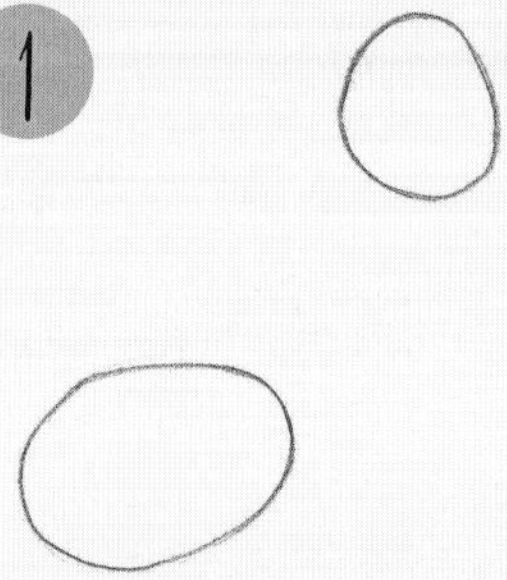

2

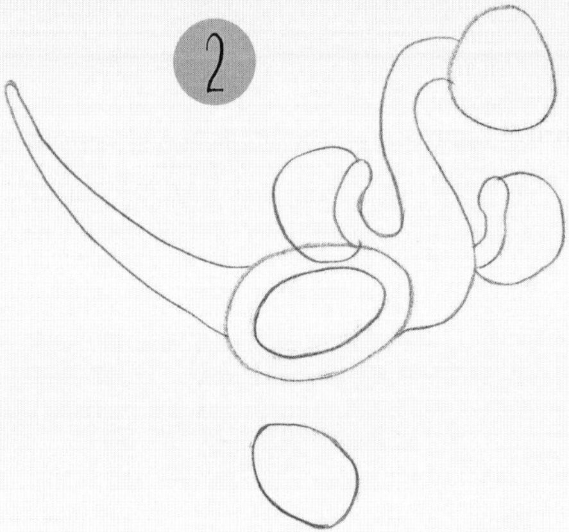

3

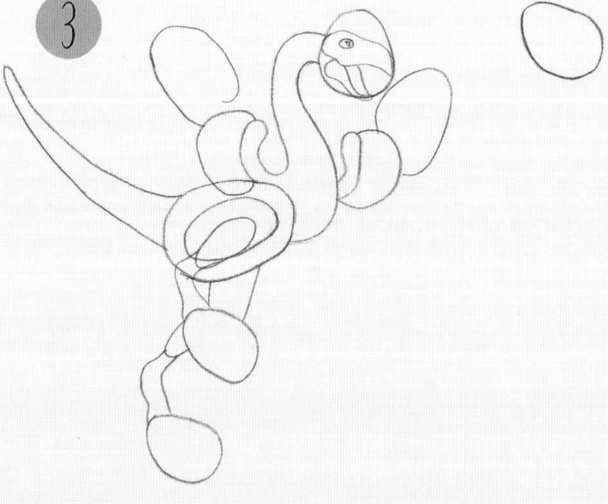

4

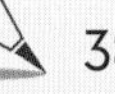

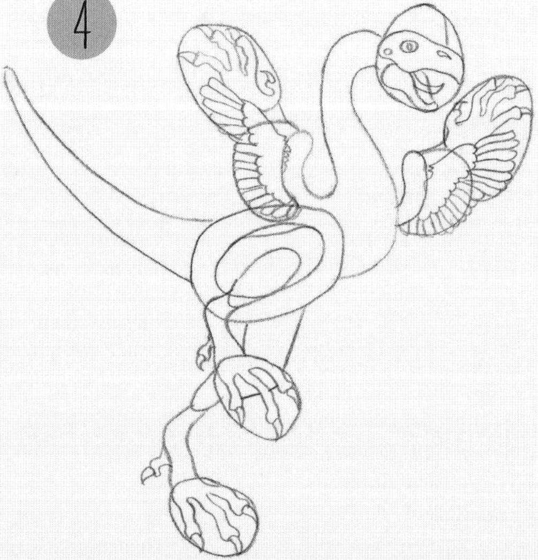

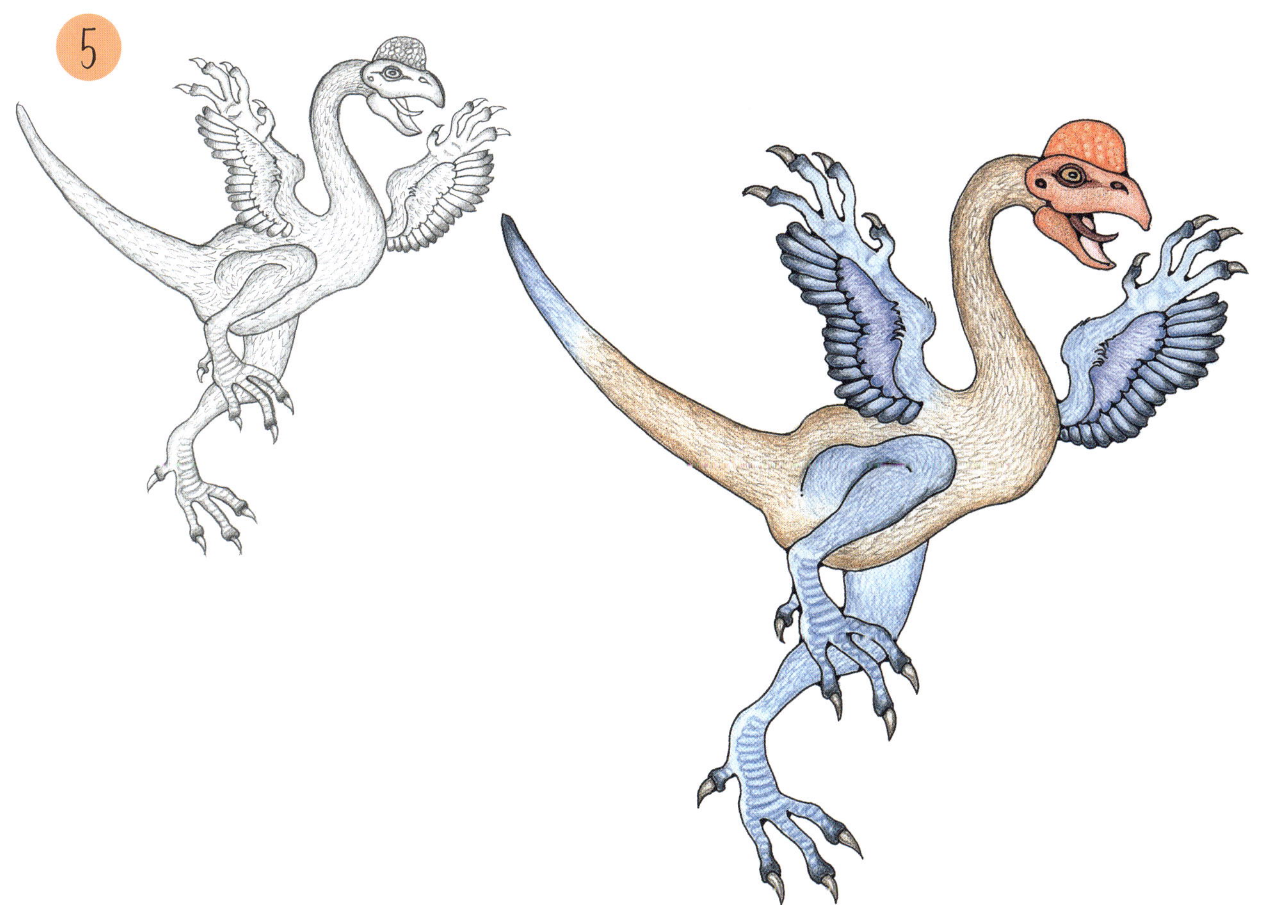
5

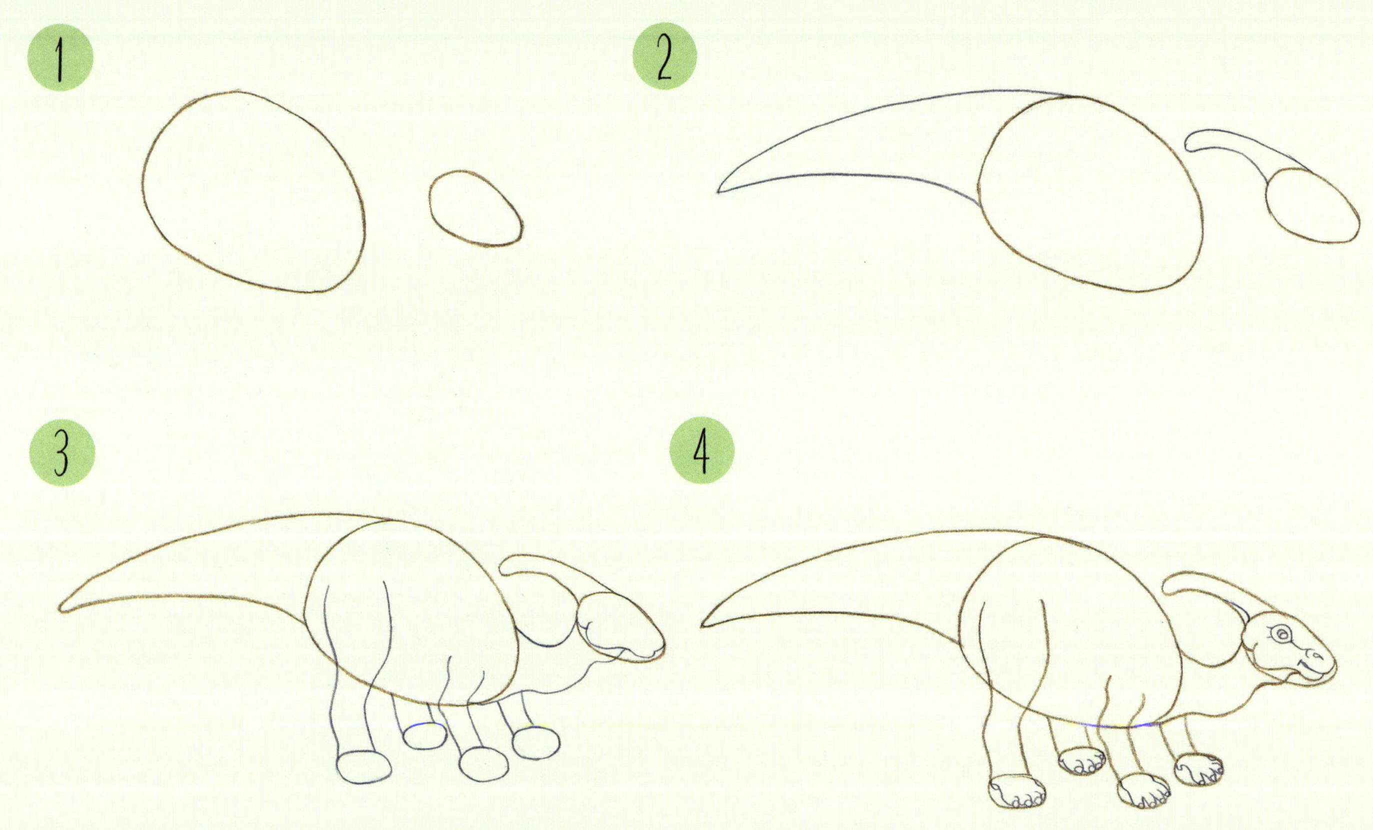
1
2
3
4

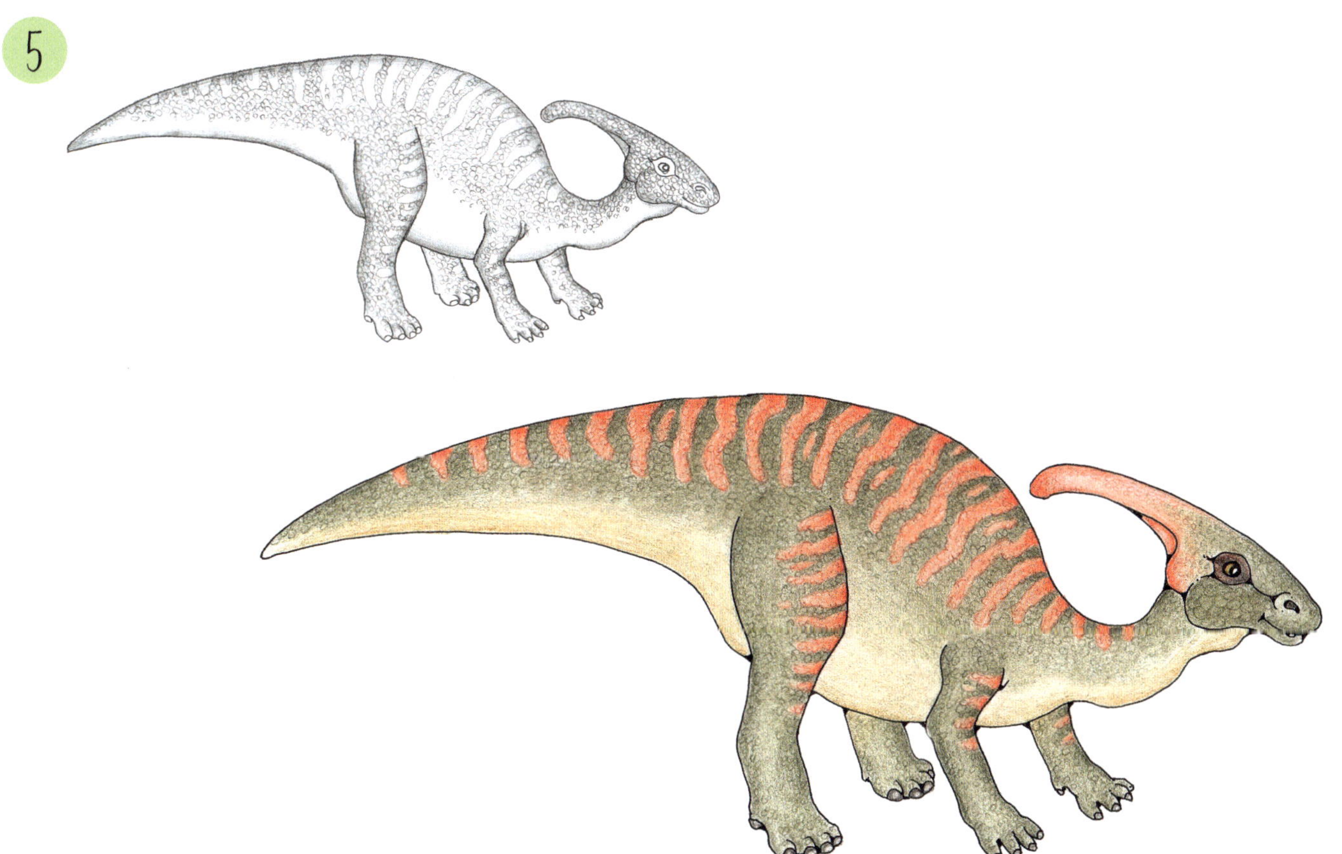
5

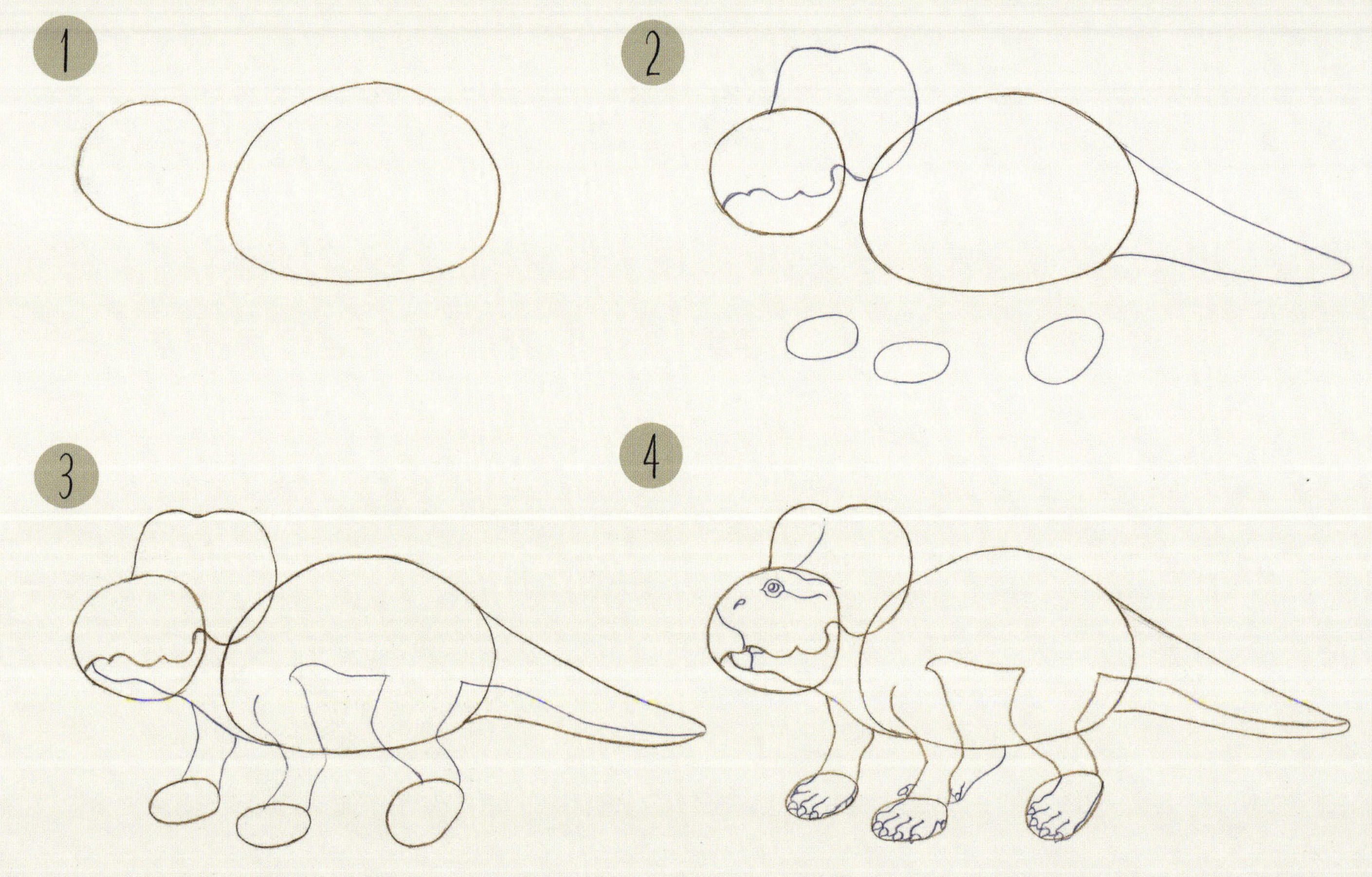
1
2
3
4

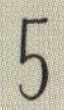

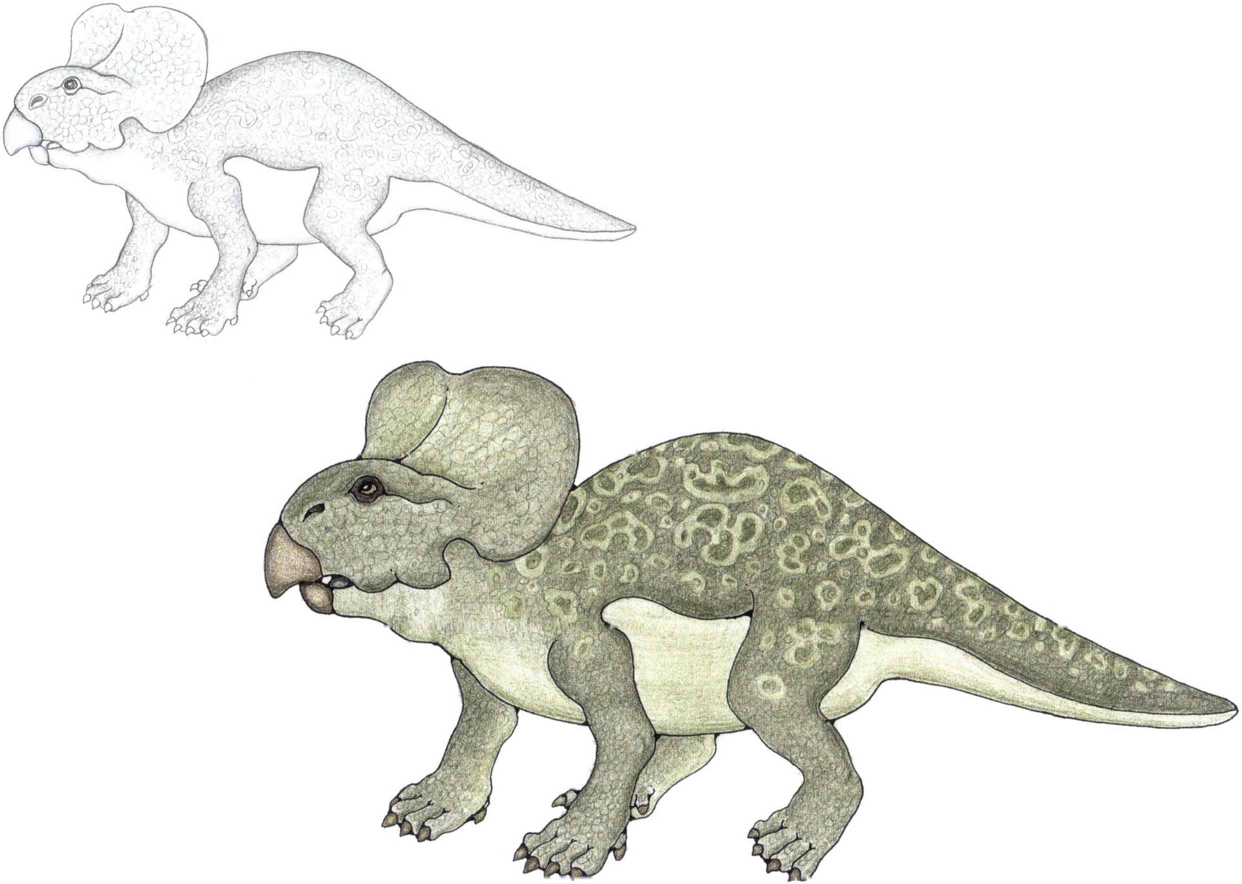

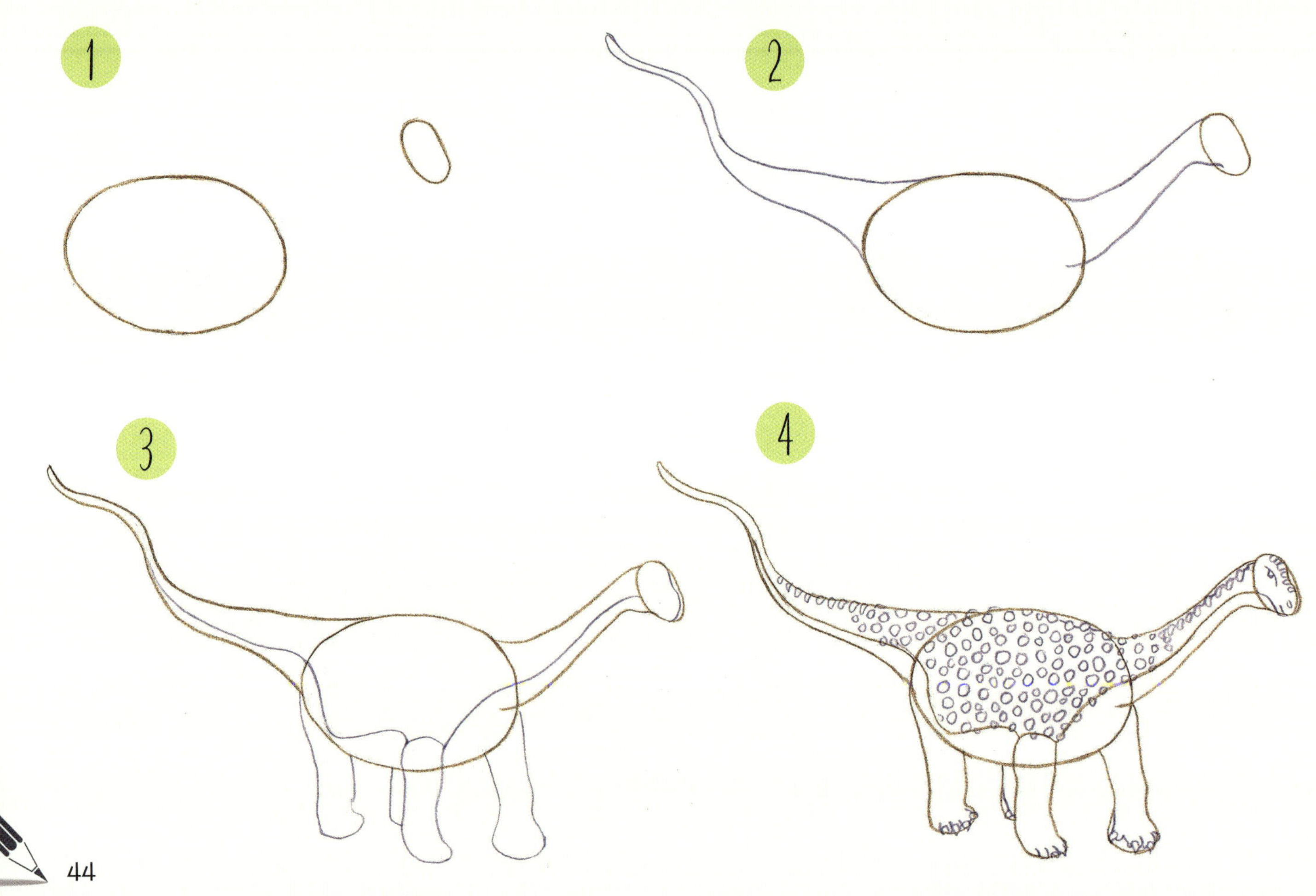
1
2
3
4

5

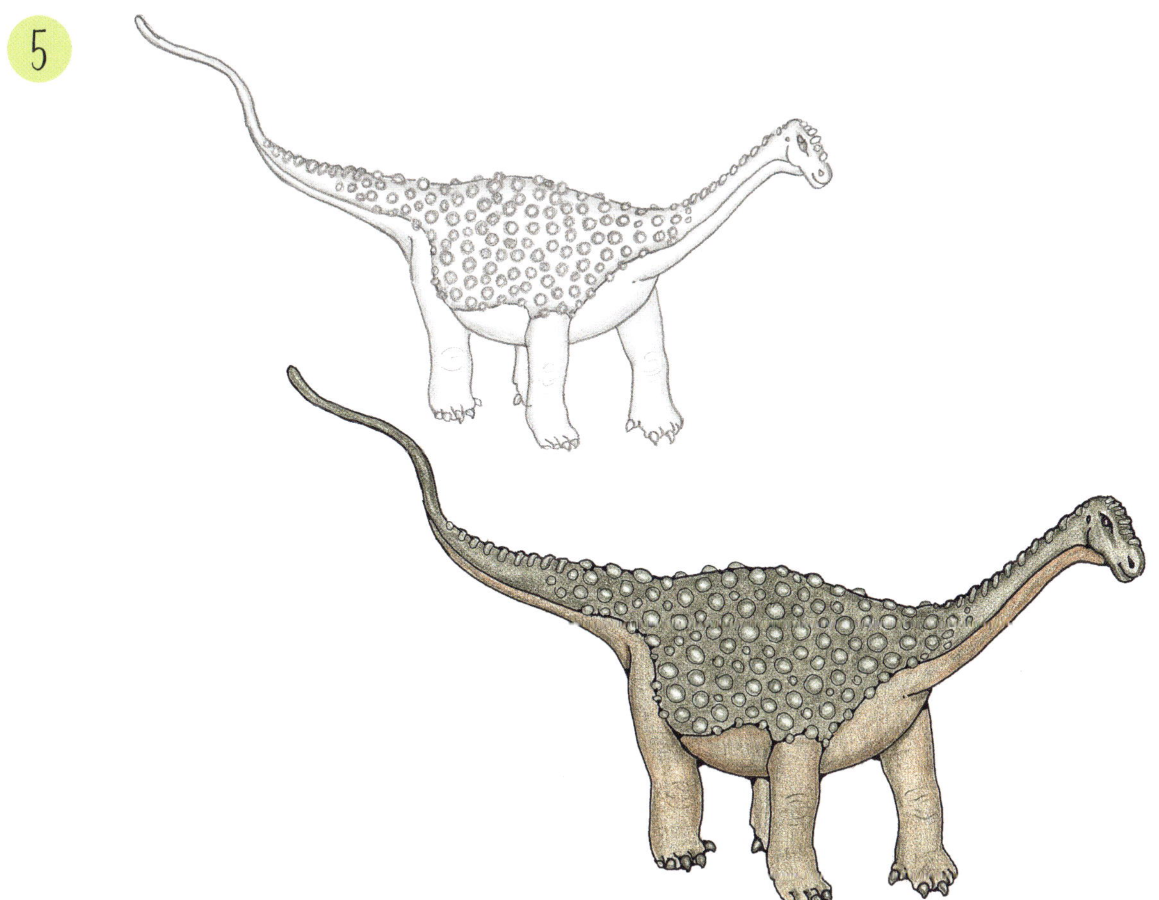

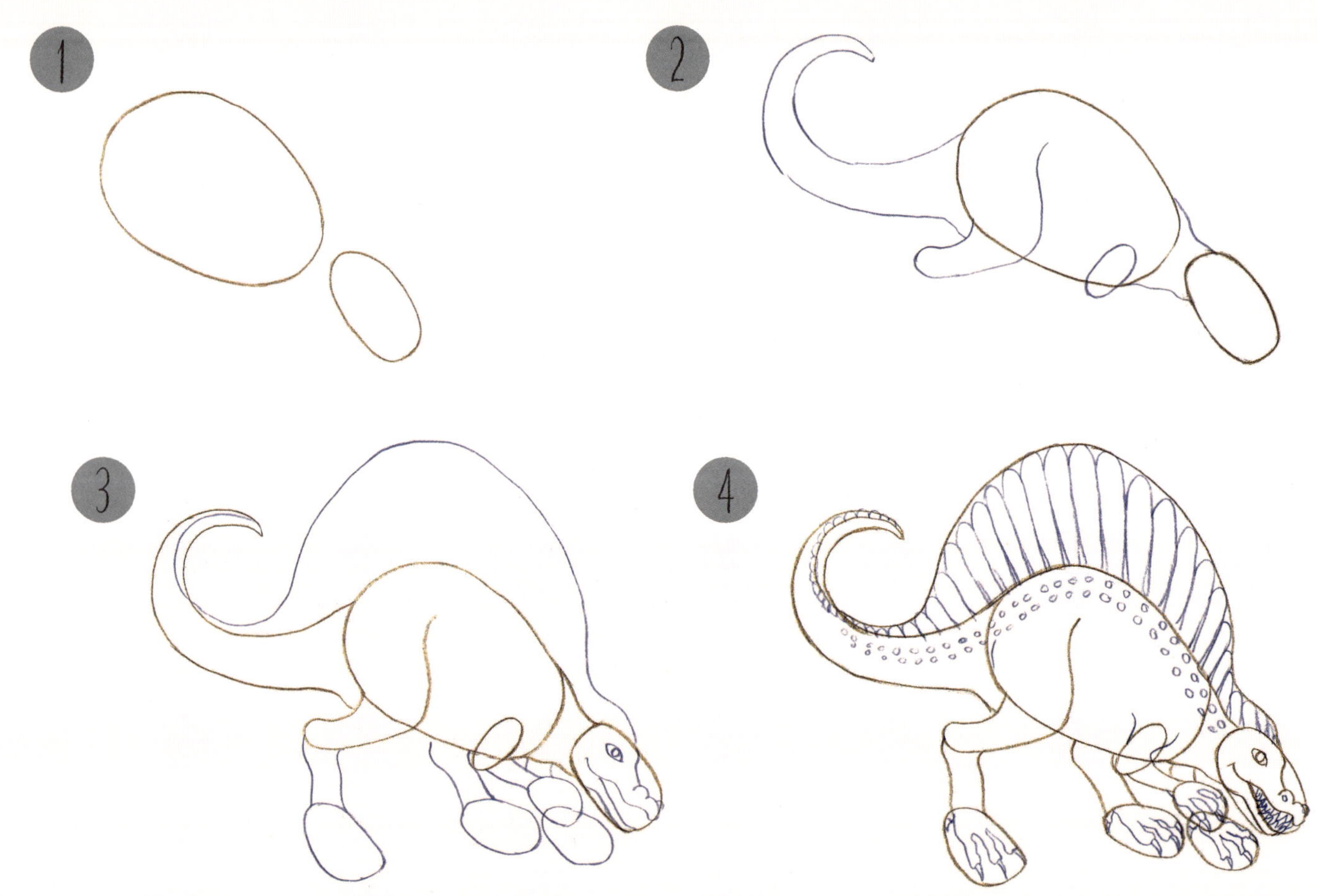
1
2
3
4

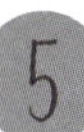
5

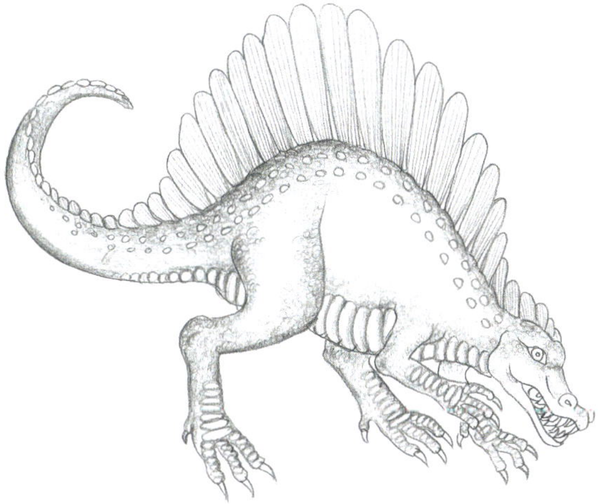

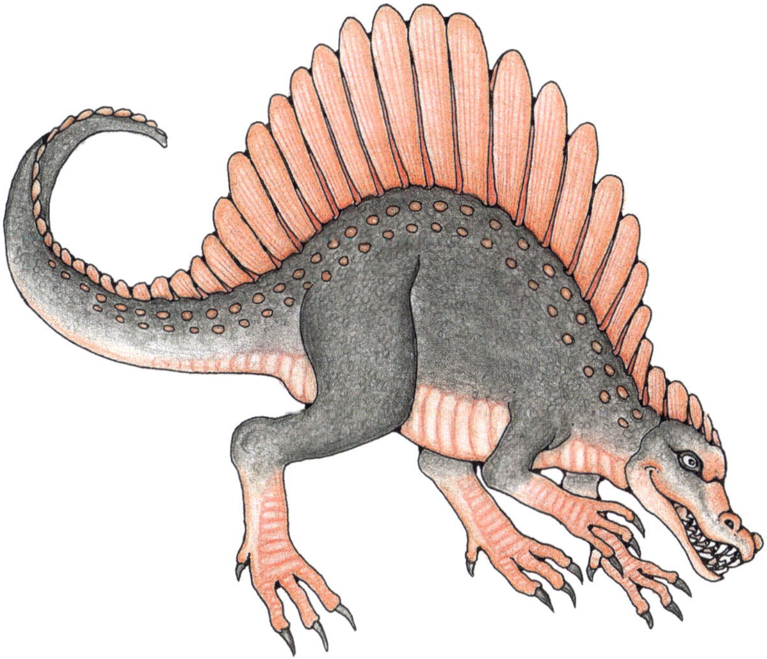

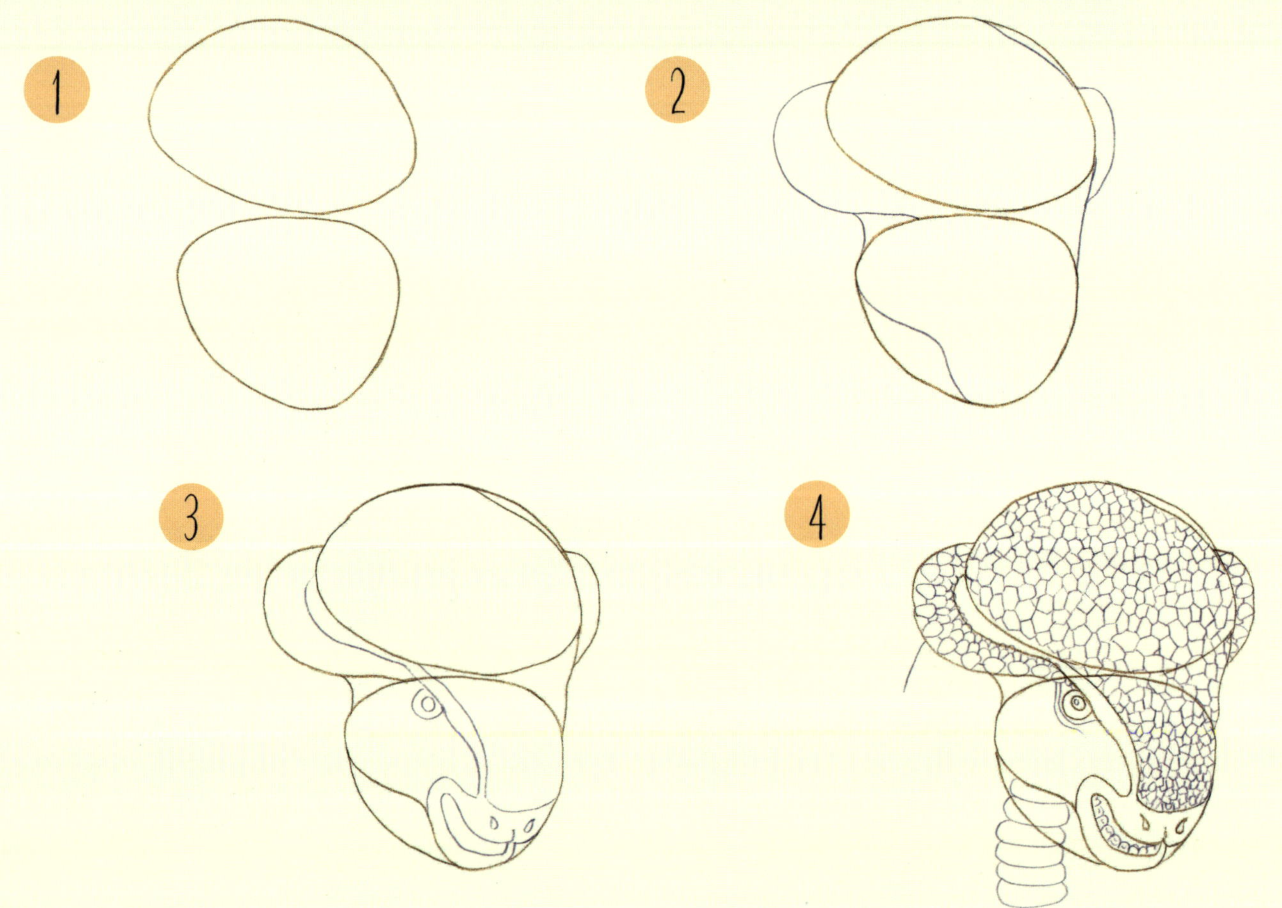
1
2
3
4

5

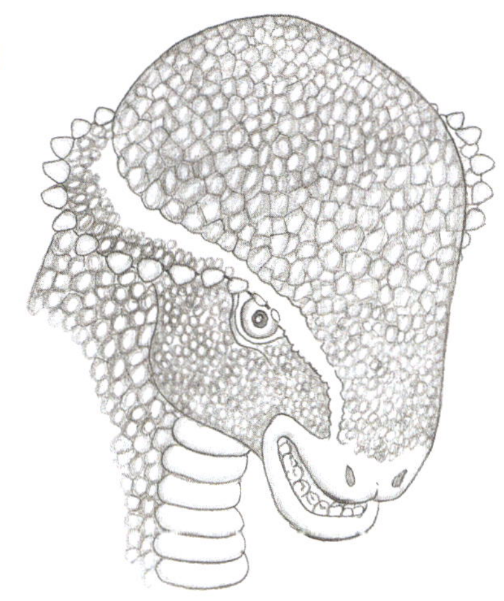

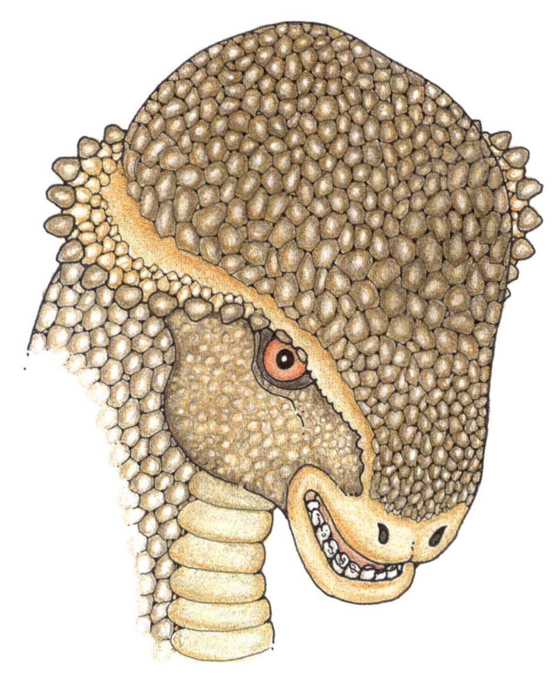

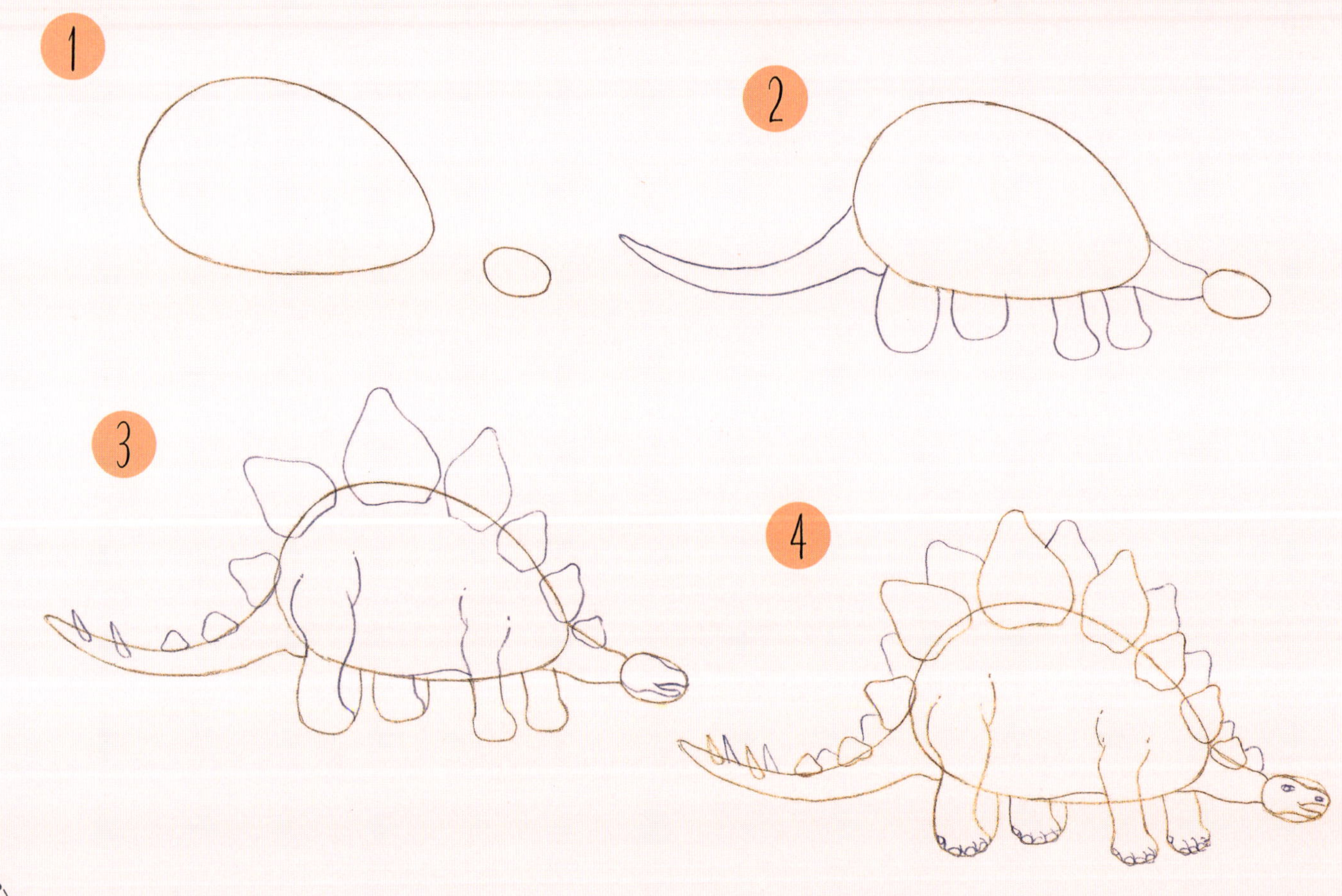
1
2
3
4

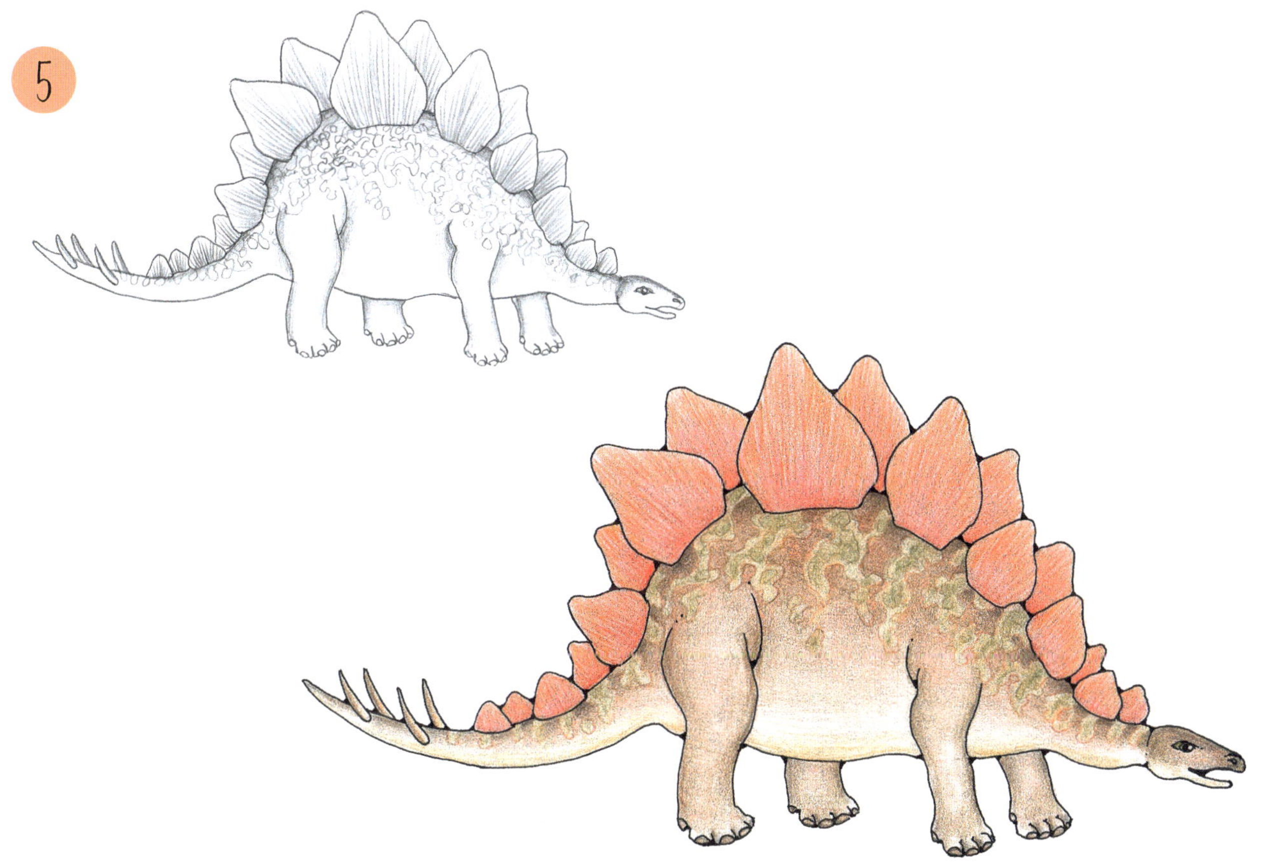
5

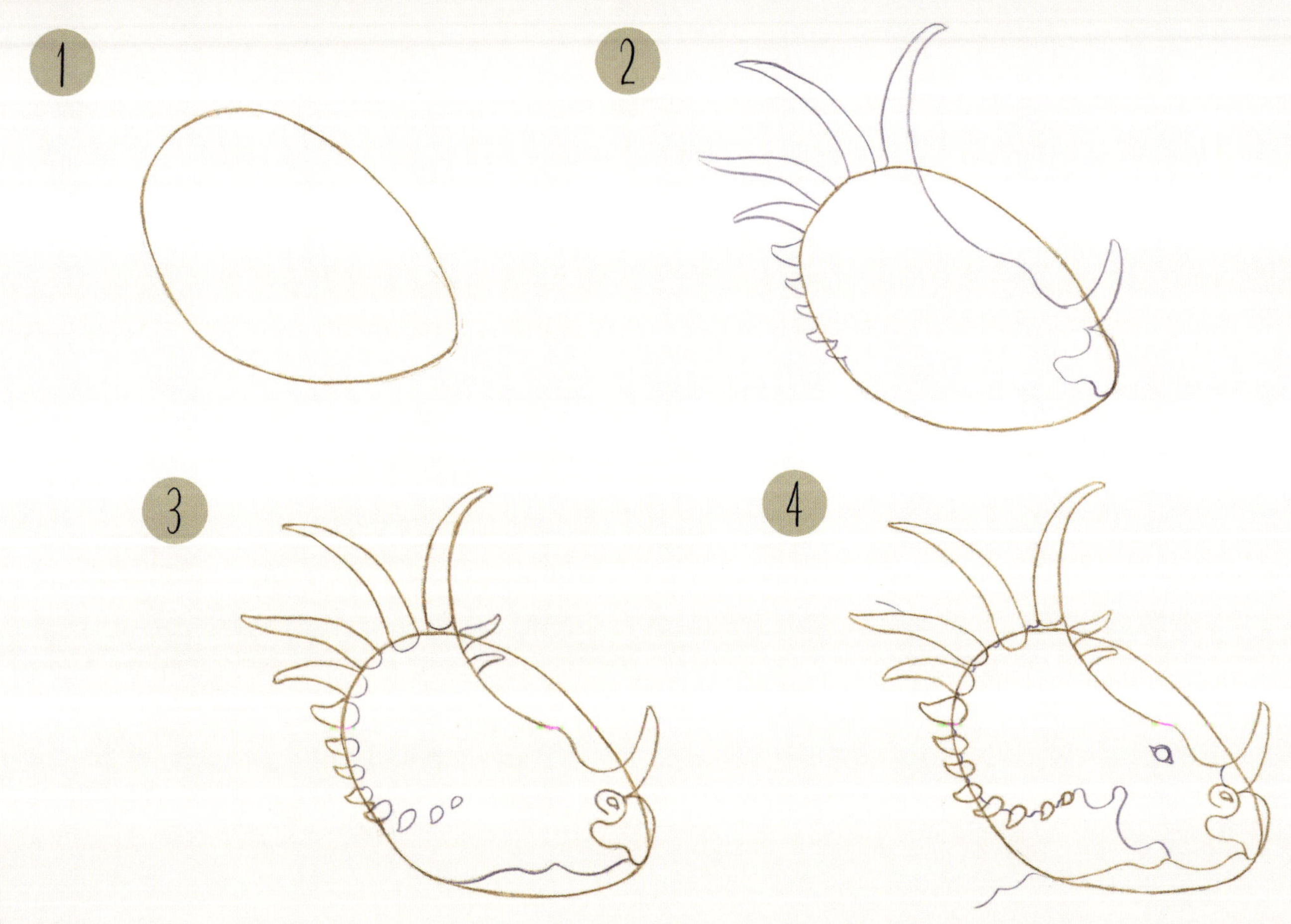
1
2
3
4

5

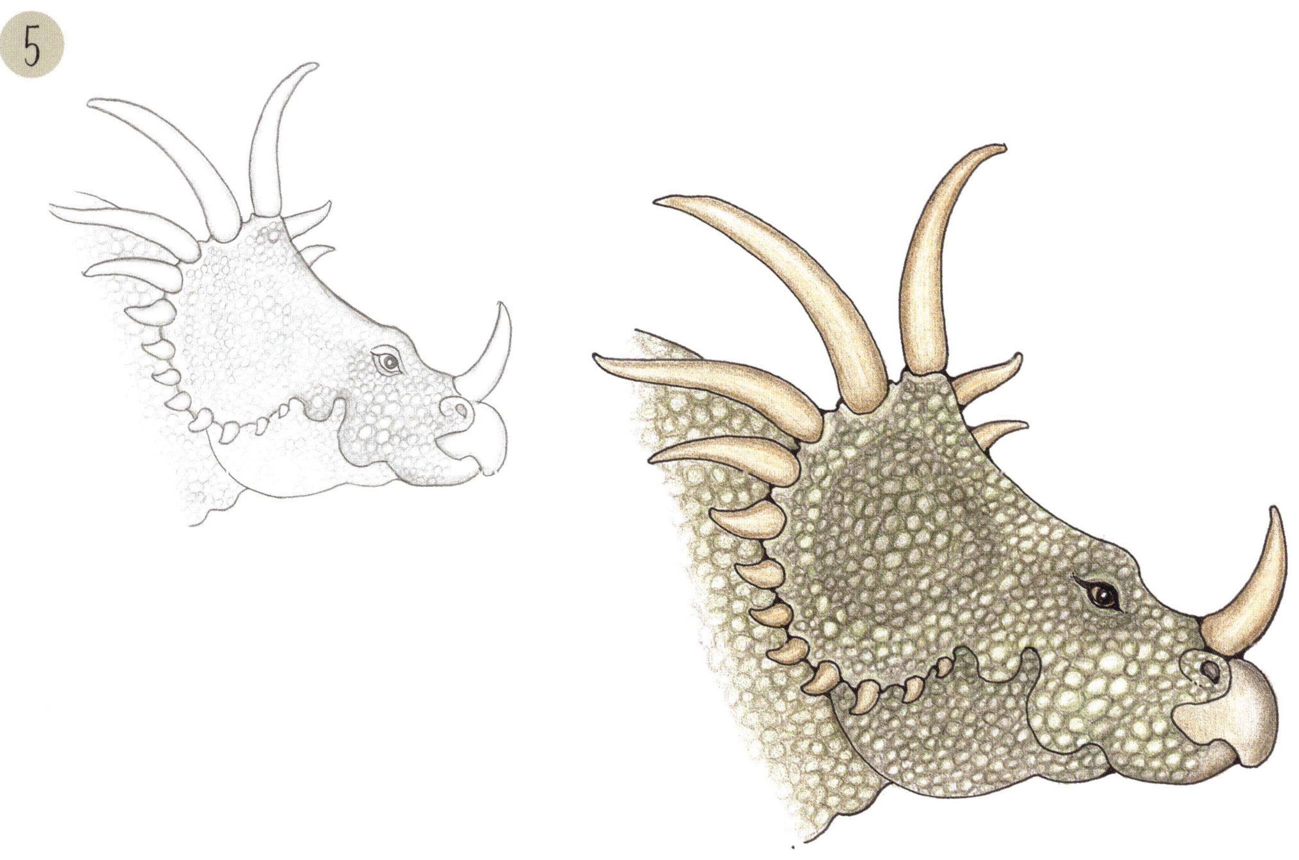

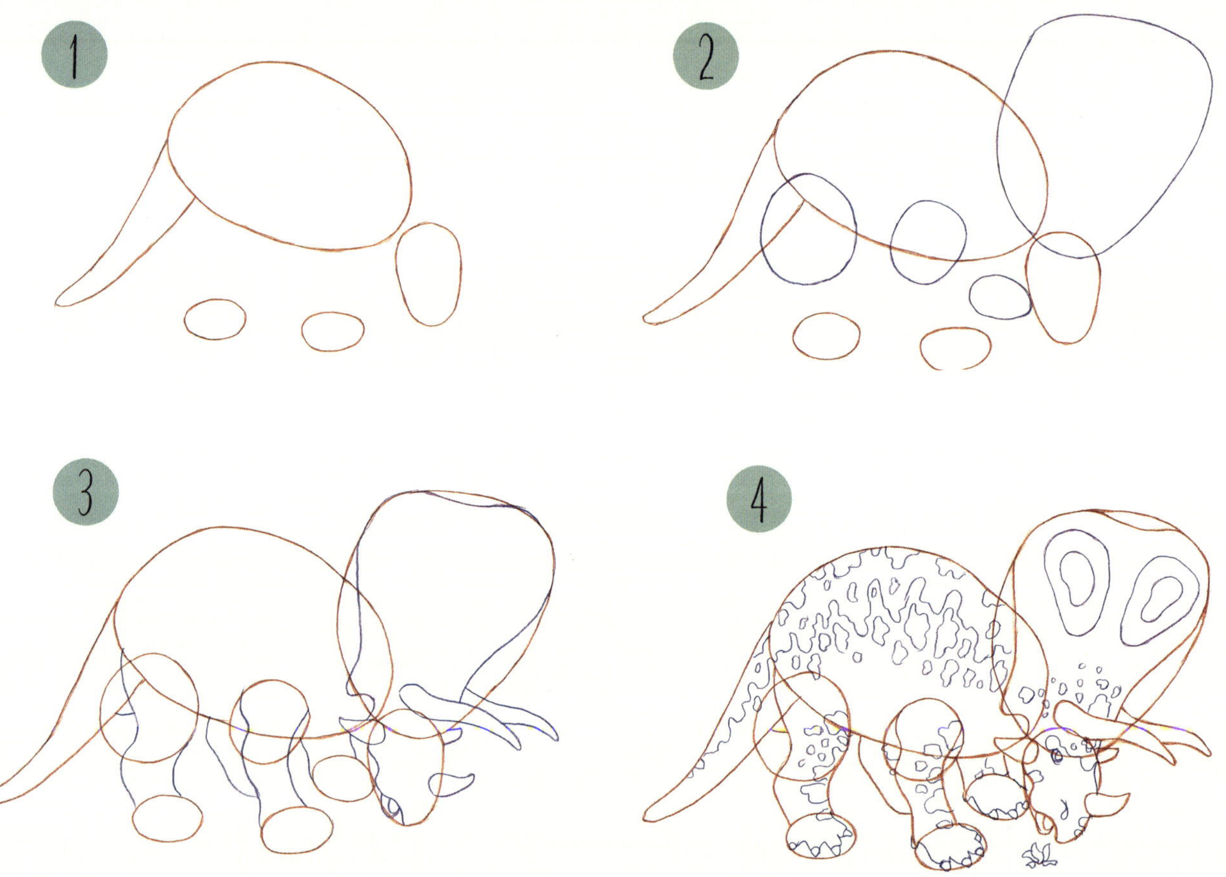
1
2
3
4

5

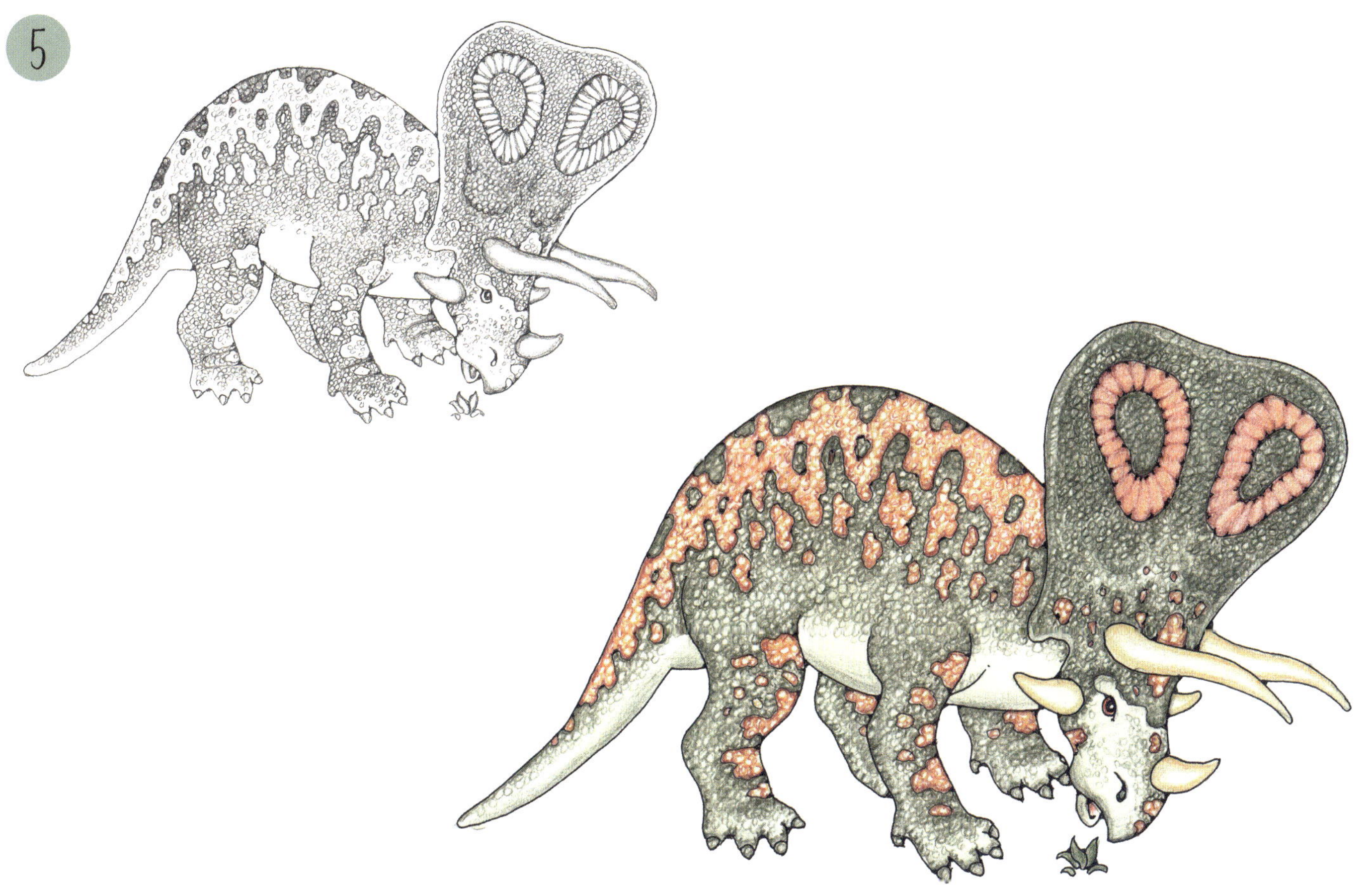

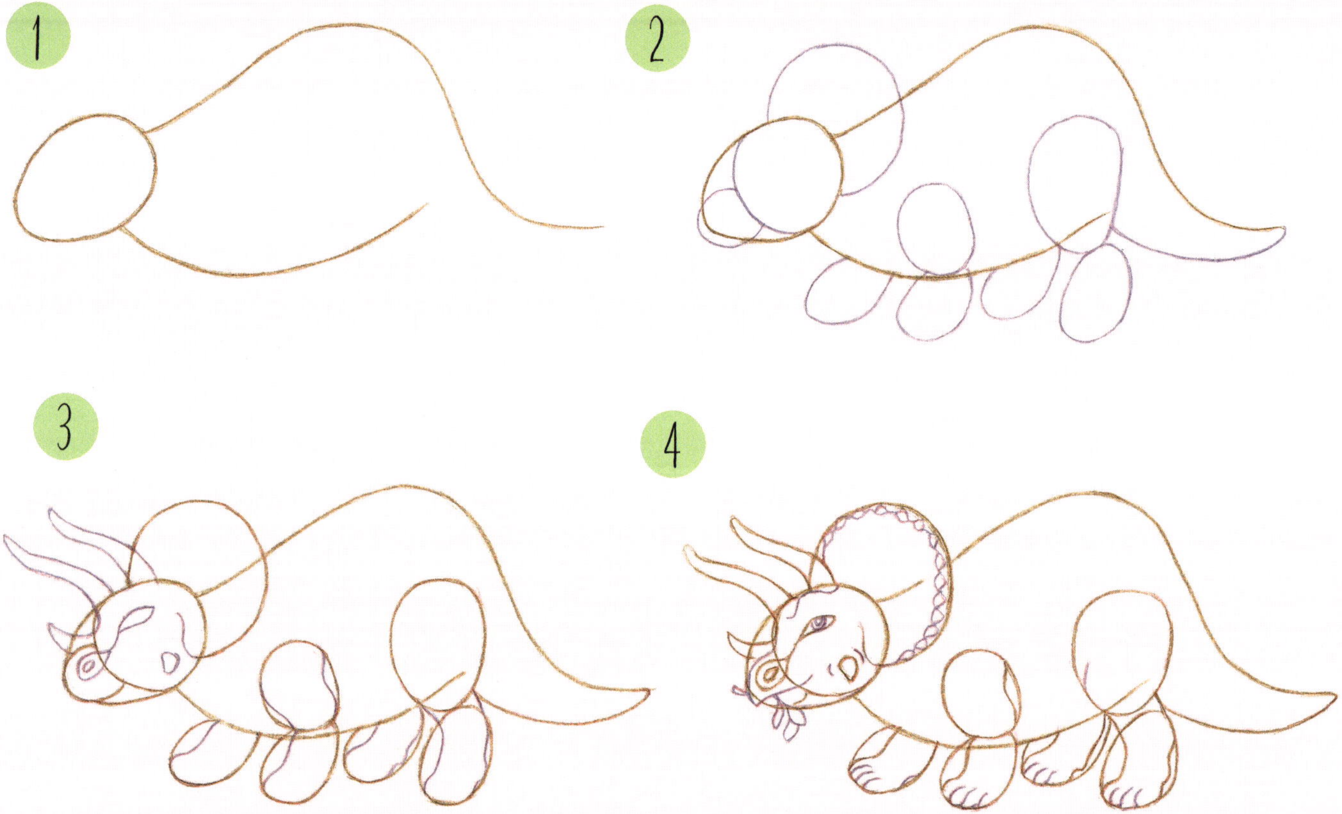

1

2

3

4

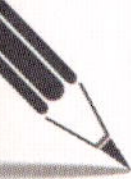

5

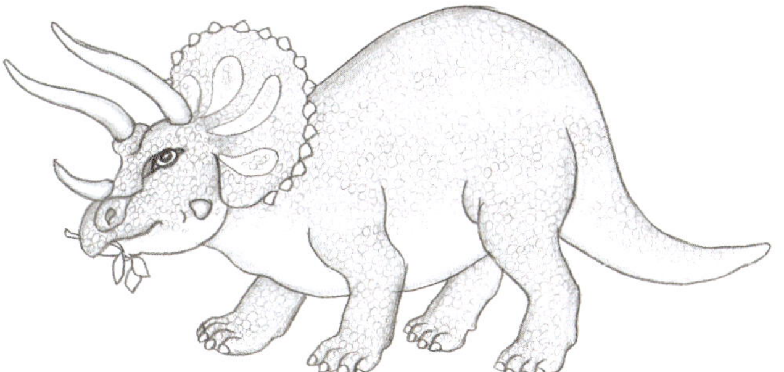

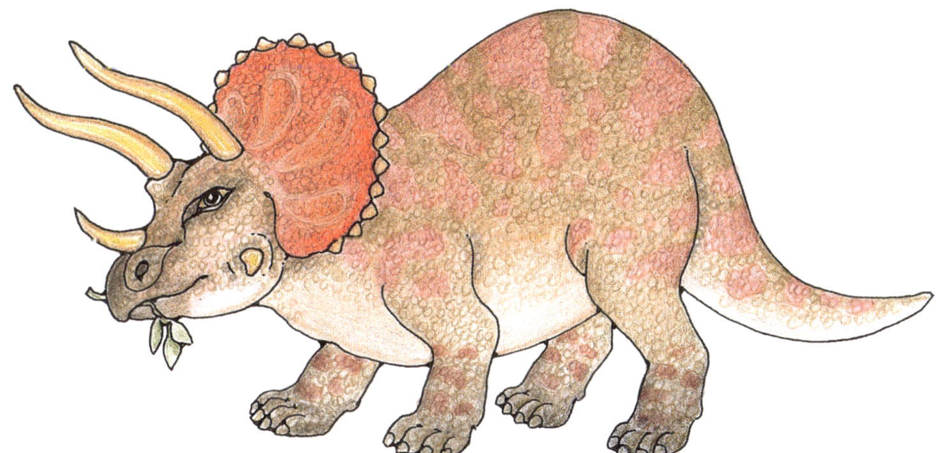

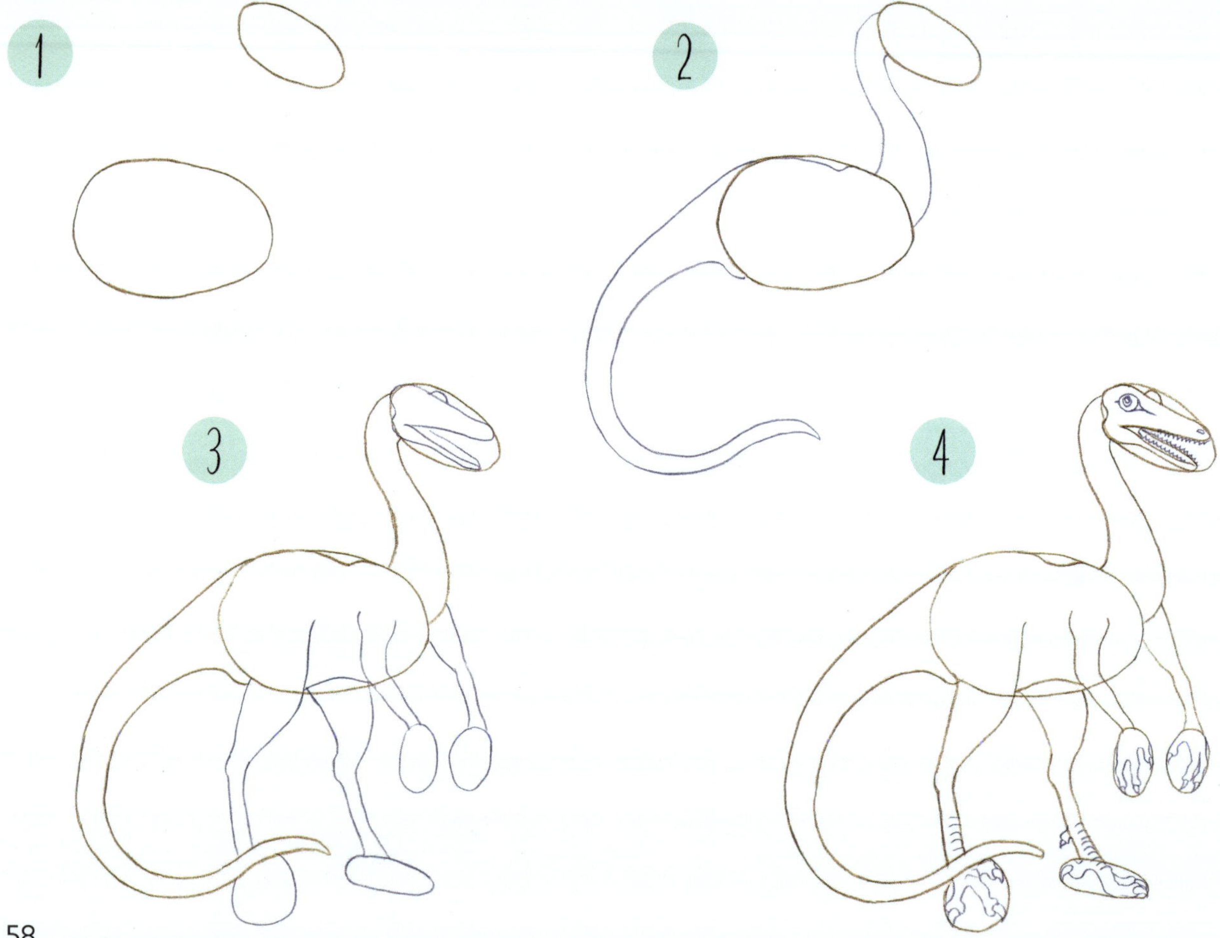
1
2
3
4

5

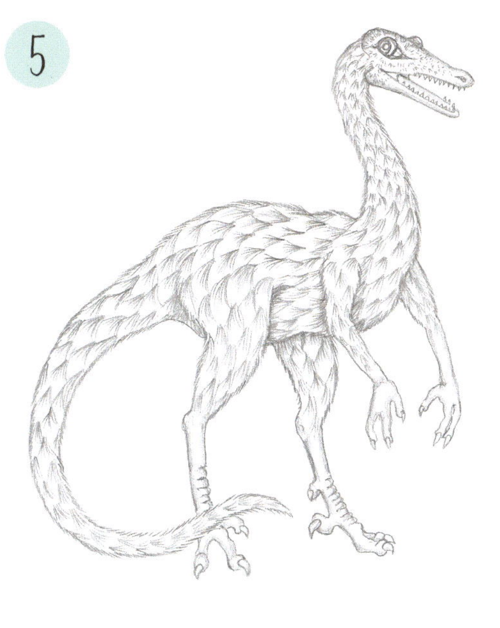

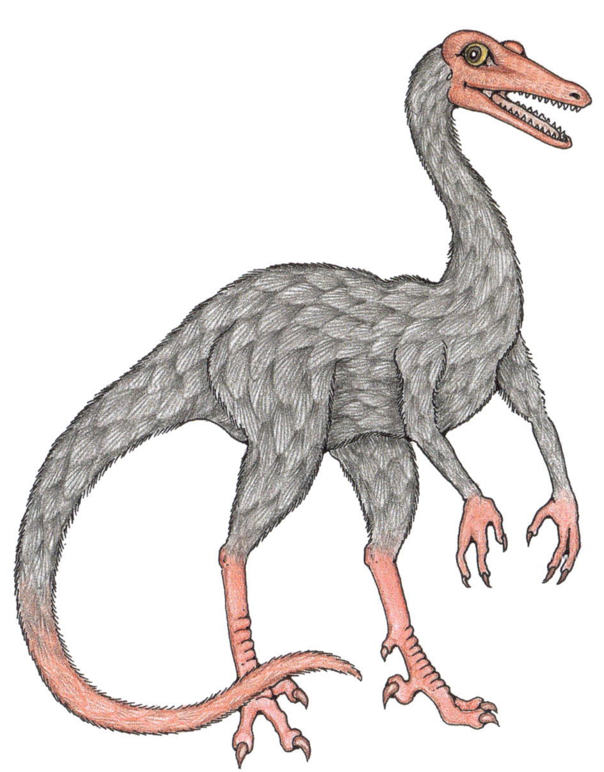

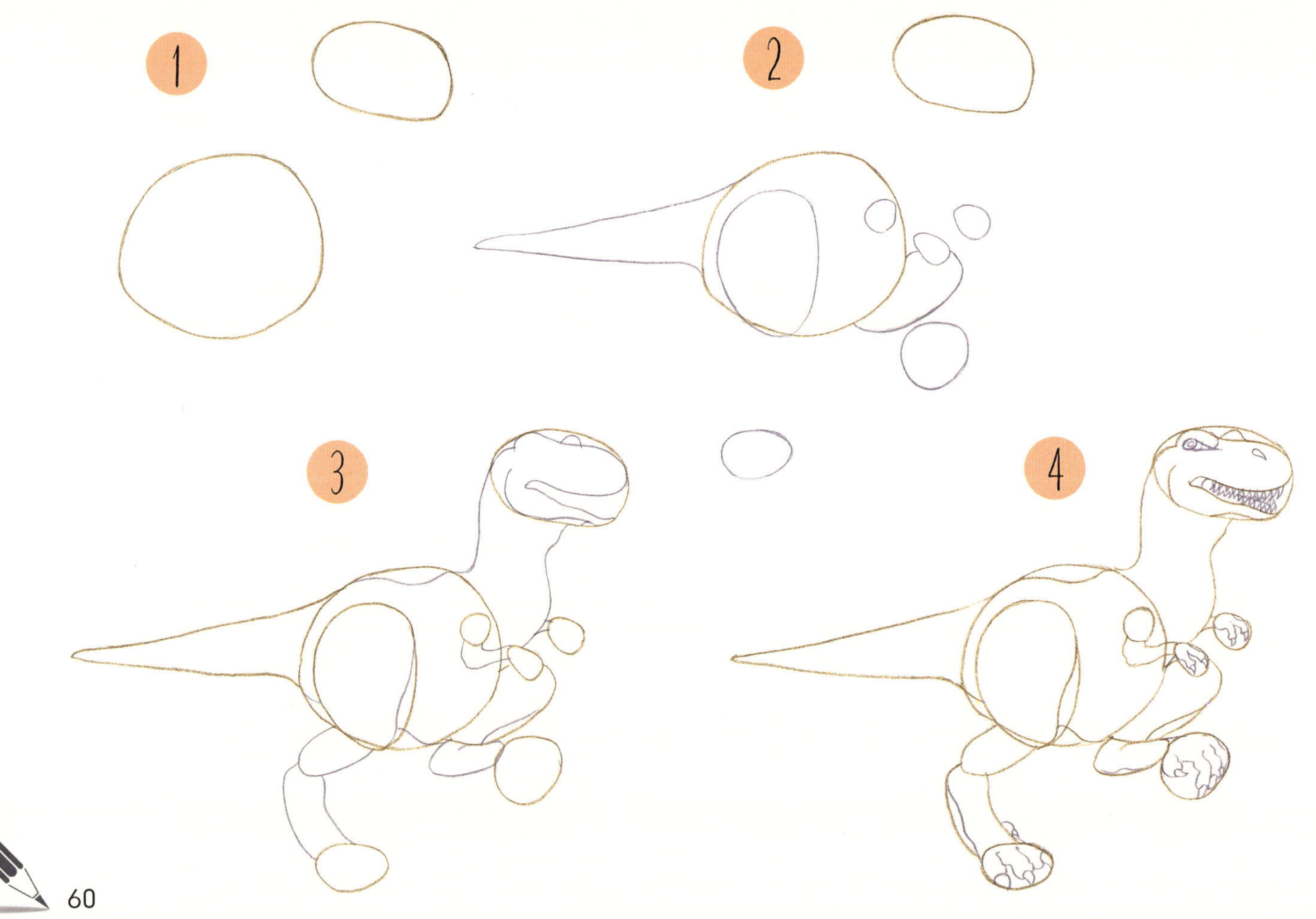
1
2
3
4

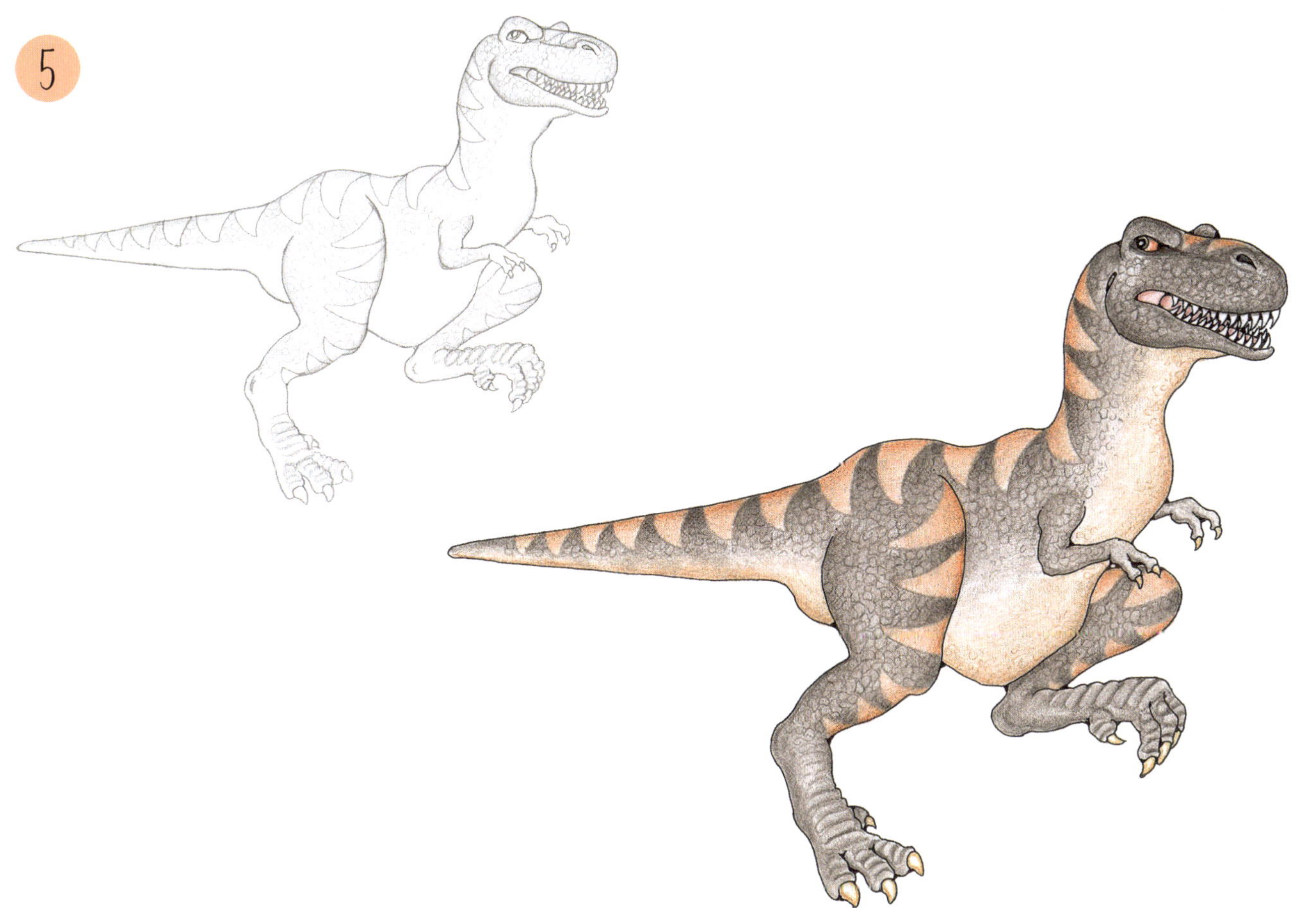
5

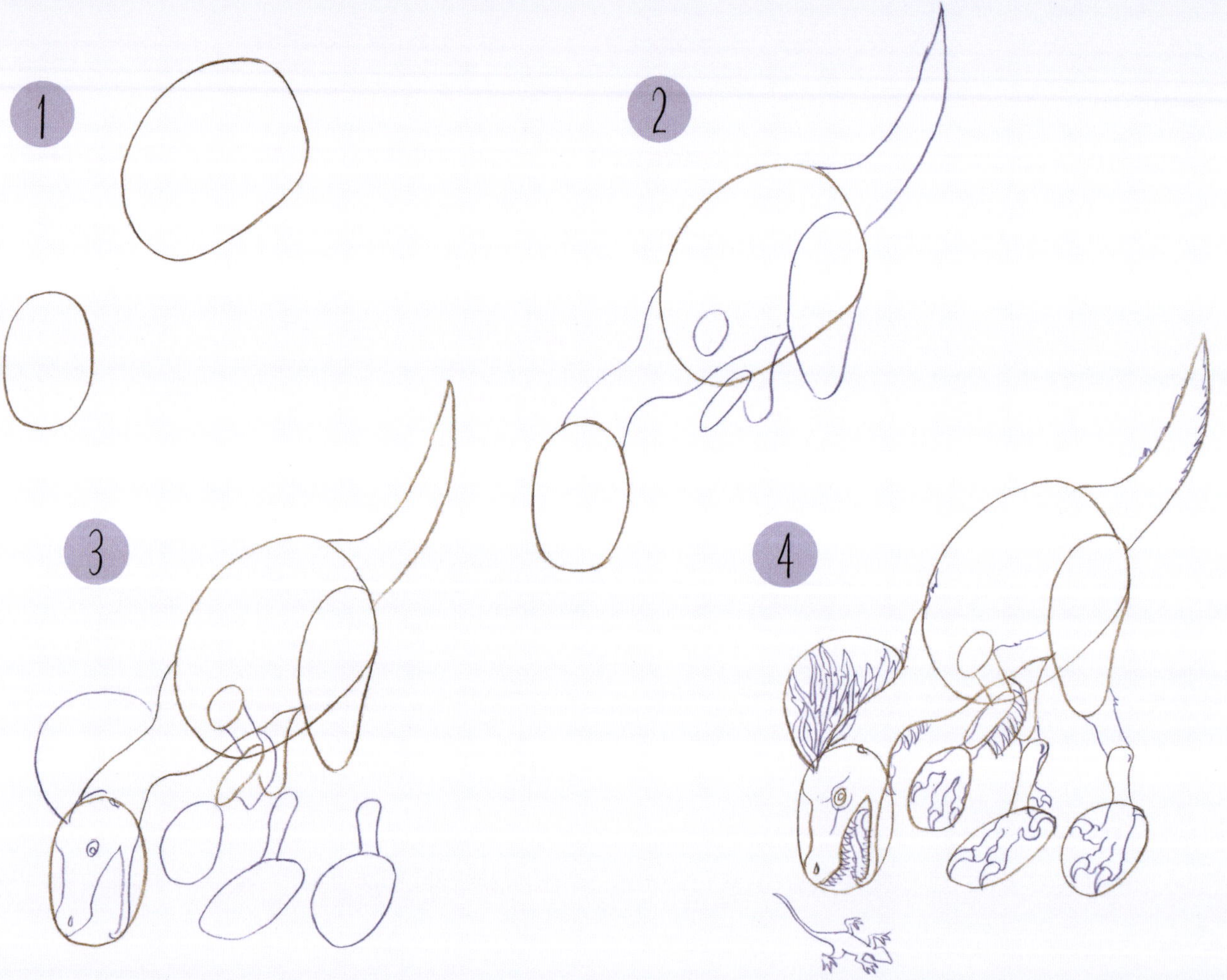

1

2

3

4

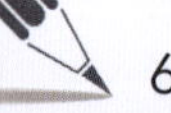

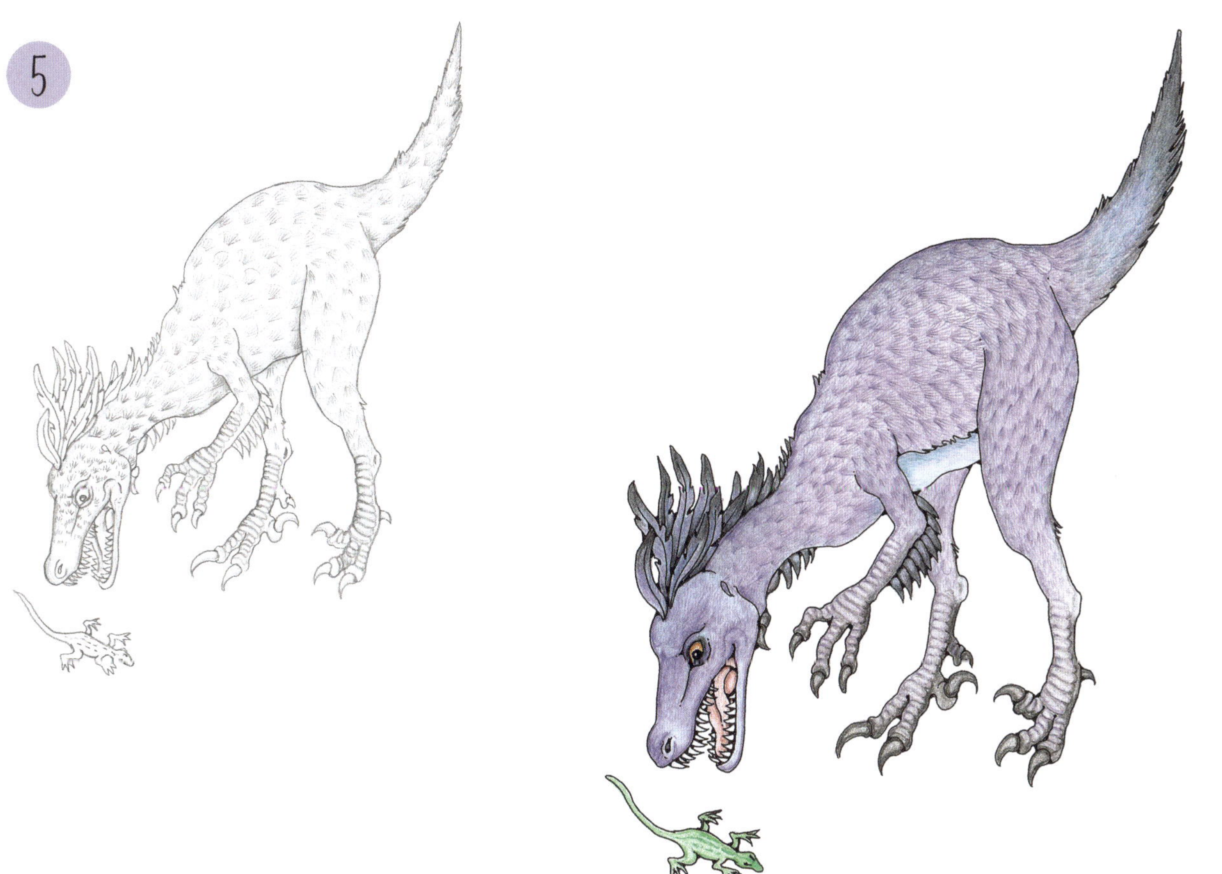
5

First published in 2026

This book includes material previously published in:
How to Draw: Dinosaurs, 2012

Search Press Limited
Wellwood, North Farm Road,
Tunbridge Wells, Kent TN2 3DR

1 2 3 4 5 6 7 8 9 10

ISBN: 978-1-80092-352-2
ebook ISBN: 978-1-80093-335-4

Bookmarked Hub
For further ideas and inspiration and to join our free online community, visit www.bookmarkedhub.com

GPSR information can be found at www.searchpress.com
Printed in China, TT092025

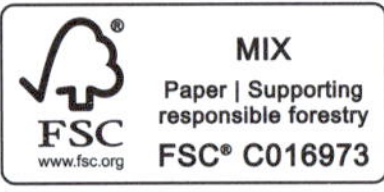

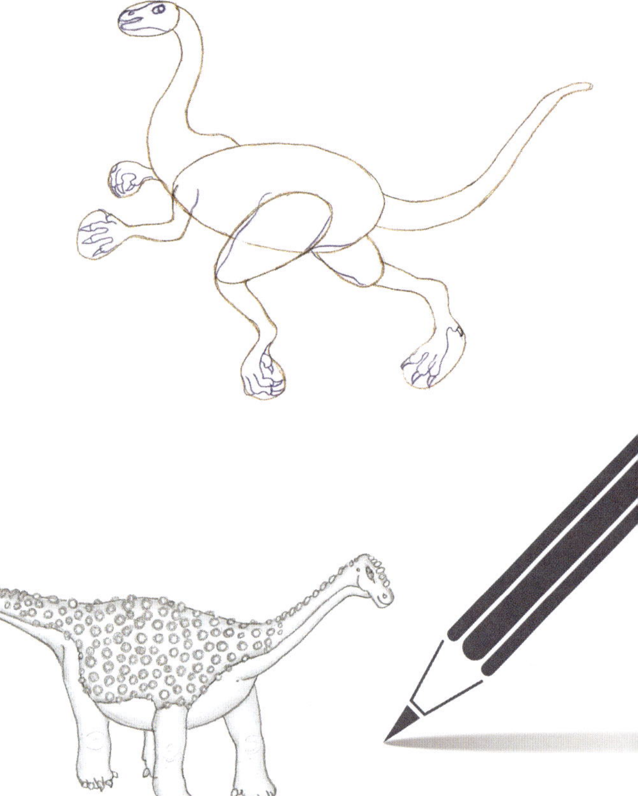